Claude

White Peak Memories

Claude Fearns

with illustrations by
Sheila Hine

ACKNOWLEDGEMENTS

I would like to thank Betty Gouldstone for her early days'
encouragement to write my memories and stories down.

My thanks also to:
Other friends at Hollinsclough History Live Group;
Colin and Margaret Bowyer,
Staff at the Honeycomb Centre, Longnor,
Telecottage, Warslow;
Frances Ward
at Derbyshire Rural Community Council.

And a thank you to all who have kindly lent photos:
Ruth Brown;
Mrs E. Clowes;
David Gould;
Muriel and Fred Hunt;
Victor and Christine Mellor;
The Swindell Family;
Jack Took;
Dennis and Jennifer Wheeldon;
Alison Wilton.

CHURNET VALLEY BOOKS
1 King Street, Leek. ST13 5NW. 01538 399033

www.thebookshopleek.co.uk

© Claude Fearns, Sheila Hine and Churnet Valley Books 2003
ISBN 1904546 04 8

Printed in England by The Bath Press

CONTENTS

THE BURRS

Chelmorton church - see page 138 for the weather vane on the top

Hard times

Way back at the beginning of my memory I can remember being in a large building, my Mum and Dad sitting with me on a long bench. There was fruit on the windowsill in front of me - apples, oranges, bananas, pears and grapes. I was very annoyed at not being able to help myself to the feast. I later realised it had been Harvest Festival at King Sterndale Church. It must have been 1929

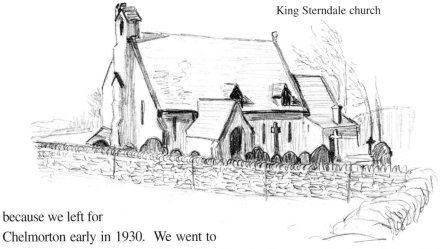

King Sterndale church

because we left for
Chelmorton early in 1930. We went to
live at Buxton House Farm with the Bagshaw family, consisting then of Mr and Mrs Bagshaw, David and Mavis. They let us use part of their farm house at Chelmorton.

I do not remember a lot of that part of my life. I was told that Mavis and I shared a pram together. I can remember Mrs Bagshaw taking Mum, Mavis and myself for a long walk to Wheeldon Trees to see her father and mother. Mavis and I had to share the pushchair, one riding a bit, then walking a bit, while the other had the ride. I did not like all the walking.

Another trip out was to Flagg Races. All I can remember of that was a red and white striped catering tent where we bought tea, sandwiches and cake.

Then, on Saturdays, Mum and I sometimes went into Buxton to do some shopping on a big red bus with a driver and a conductor who sold Mum a ticket from a rack he carried around with him. Before he gave Mum the ticket, he put it into a contraption with a bell on it, which rang as a hole was punched in the ticket. In Buxton, we bought some butter and a large brown Hovis loaf to eat at Mrs Dawson's house with a cup of tea she made for us. She was a lovely old person - poor but proud. If we had taken groceries for her she would not have accepted them, but she would allow us to leave uneaten bread and butter behind. Butter was weighed from bulk and you could have what weight you asked for. We made sure that Mrs Dawson was left with a good lump of butter and three quarters of a large loaf; it was the only way to help her out and repay her kindness to us.

Another trip I vaguely remember was when Ma, Muriel, Joyce and I once went with Sunday School to Southport on a coach from Chelmorton. We did not see the sea but spent some time round the pleasure beach. Muriel and Joyce got a very large stuffed doll each.

We left Buxton House when I was three and moved to an old house further down the village, with an outbuilding in which my father used to repair and sell bicycles. He also gave short sharp haircuts to anyone brave enough, for threepence a time. He worked in the limestone quarries when there was work to be had - anything to earn a shilling - or did casual farm work as the seasons required, like muck spreading, paid as

My sisters, Muriel and Joyce, at the Burrs.

piece work at sixpence a score. Times were hard but we survived alright. I had some good times and some good friends at Chelmorton. The Robinsons, Morris, Donald and Margaret, lived straight across the road, and the Rileys were down the road a bit.

Mr Stanway used to deliver fish once a week with an old car with a platform on the back half. He stopped at intervals on his way through the village to serve customers. Now, we used to have a big cat called Thomas who was very fond of fish, and he would watch out for the car, jump on the back, steal a fish in a flash and make his escape, always chased by anyone handy. If the cat dropped his fish, it was grabbed by his pursuers, taken home, washed and used. Thomas would sometimes have to stalk the cart all the way up the village to finally get his prize.

Mr Wilton came round twice a week with green groceries on a flat horse cart. I remember that horse well. It was a beautiful, half-legged chestnut with a dark mane and tail.

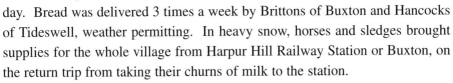

We had no tap water in the house so all the water had to be carried from a cast iron stand-pipe, using a key to turn it on and off. Electricity had not reached the village either, so we used paraffin lamps. Hardware and lamp oil were delivered by Mr Shaw with his horse and cart.

Milk was also delivered but you had to take a jug and meet a horse and float and have your milk taken from a churn and put into the jug with a pint measure once a day. Bread was delivered 3 times a week by Brittons of Buxton and Hancocks of Tideswell, weather permitting. In heavy snow, horses and sledges brought supplies for the whole village from Harpur Hill Railway Station or Buxton, on the return trip from taking their churns of milk to the station.

When I was four, we moved again, this time to The Burrs, a small farm which my grandfather owned, while he had moved to a very big farm himself.

Tony Chapman.

Mavis's Auntie Gladys from
Wheeldon Trees.

Mr Ted Grindey.

The good in things

The day we moved to the Burrs was the worst day of my young life. Being over a mile away from my friends, with no road or contact with them, it might as well have been a hundred. How we moved, I don't know. The furniture would have to go by horse and cart. I do remember that my mother, Mrs Pickford and I walked. I didn't realise at the time that we were moving to live there.

As soon as the penny dropped I was horrified and kicked up something shocking. My mother was trying to piece together the oilcloth from the old house and lay it on the floor. Knowing I loved to tinker with a hammer and nails, she got me a small hammer and a tin lid of nails so I could help her. But I was so mad I took the nails and hammer and pushed them out of reach under one of the farm building doors.

I kept this tantrum up all week until Saturday afternoon. When Father got home from work, he decided I needed to do some work. I was entrusted with collecting fire-lighting sticks - breaking dry twigs into nine inch pieces, putting them into bundles, one bundle for each morning, and setting them to dry over the oven. The weekend spent with my father did me a lot of good.

Now, in this little job of mine there was a lot more than met the eye. Since there were only five trees round the yard, the supply of dead wood soon dried up, so I had to go further away from home for a fresh supply. Looking around, I could see one tree in the small garden about 200 yards and two walls away; the walls put me off that straightaway. There was another in the top stable field, a little further off but with no walls to get over. But yet another tree, in the big meadow behind the farmyard, was nearer still, and with no walls to bar my way. This was obviously the best bet, so, with a basket, off I went.

On reaching the tree, things were not as straightforward as I had expected, for these twigs had thorns on them, sharp, nasty spikes which pricked and scratched. But with more respect and careful handling, I managed to fill my quota. Standing there, feeling pleased with myself for my efforts, I took a good look at this tree. It was the kind of tree to be avoided if possible. Its bark and shape was different from the others in the farmyard, so I looked back at those kinder trees, then looked for others like them in shape and colour.

Yes, the one in the garden and the one in the stable field were the same and further out, at the top of the field I was in, was another of the same kind and shape, but it was over the wall in someone else's ground, very close but just over the boundary. I could also see two small round woods with my kind of trees in them, out of bounds to me again. What had seemed like a dull job collecting firewood was turning into an adventure and a source of valuable knowledge for myself.

I could not wait for Dad to get home from work to tell him what I had found out for myself. With it being Friday, Dad worked late at the quarry, filling Saturday morning's quota of stone, so I had gone to bed when he got home. But when he saw the kind of fire lighting sticks drying on top of the oven, he knew where I had been for them. The next morning he called me from bed early and I was delighted to find he wasn't going to work. I told him about the nasty tree in the big meadow. Being a nice morning he said, *"We'll go and have a closer look at this tree of yours."* He got two pieces of light rope, a short one for me and a long one for him, and off we went, complete with a handy saw.

Getting up to the thorn tree, he said, *"Well you've found the bad in it, now let's look for the good. The leaves we can eat, the blossoms we can make good wine with, the berries will help to feed our friends, the birds, in winter; it gives good shelter and when it dies it is the best wood for baking with because hawthorn burns very hot. Always look for the good in all things and you won't go far wrong".* I've thought about that tree many times through my life.

Leaving the thorn tree behind, we moved to the top end of the meadow to where a number of tree branches hung over into our side, dropping a nice few wind-blown twigs and branches over the wall. Dad began to cut the larger timber into six-foot lengths, lying them across his piece of doubled rope. We put the smaller pieces on my rope. When it was finished and all laid tidy, he pushed the two loose ends of the rope through the double ends, pulling the sticks into a neat bundle ready to put on his back. Then he did the same for me, with my sticks.

"Well," he said, *"That's this little lot cleared up. Next, we must put back any stones which have fallen off the walls."*

"So, where's your next move for firewood?" *"Well,"* I said, *" there's that one in the garden and the one in the stable field. From the look, they're the*

same as this and those in the yard." "Very good," he said. I could see he was pleased with my observations. *"And then what? Come on, what else can you point out?"*

"There are the two round woods over there and some more across the tops of those fields, but whose are they?" "They belong to Mr Grindey. He'll be coming to see how we're getting on one of these days and you can ask him if he'll let you pick any fallen firewood over there too."

"And what else have you got to tell me?" "There's a big tree near to the one in the stable field". "Does that really look like the others?" Dad asked. This made me stop and look carefully. *"No, it's a lighter colour and more bushy." "Good,"* he said. *"You can save a lot of time looking carefully before you set off. That one's different. It's a lime tree and lime is no good for burning, so forget that one".* Looking further away to my right, I could see a larger rambling wood and pointing to it I asked, *"Who owns that?" "Oh, you know him, it's Mr Bagshaw."* With that, we shouldered our bundles and went home. As we got closer to the farmyard, there was a smell of frying bacon in the wind.

Sure enough, Mr Grindey, a very nice and pleasant man, turned up on Sunday morning with his little dog, Nina. She was a rough haired Jack Russell and her party piece was to sit up and sing. After praising his little dog I thought it might be the right time to discuss business, so I approached the subject of firewood lying in his fields. He said, just as normal as could be, *"It'll cost you."*

I hadn't expected this and was stuck for words. I just looked at him, so after a while he spoke again. *"There are some small stones around my mere, left over from when I cleaned it out and spread the mud on the field. I could do with them collected up and put into a nice neat heap. What do you say?"* I quickly agreed and the deal was done. During the next week I collected up all the stones but I did not dare touch the firewood until he had seen the job for himself.

Sunday came and so did Mr Grindey and he had inspected the fields on his way down. *"You have made a fine job, young man"*, he said, and then he asked if I had any hens of my own. I was puzzled but I just said, *"No"* - I thought he wanted some eggs as well as the stone picking - but no more was said.

The weeks went by and as I still had plenty of wood to go at I hadn't touched that in his fields. Another Sunday morning arrived and was foggy but Mr Grindey and Nina arrived at the Burrs as usual. He looked at me and said,

Chelmorton from Pippinwell Lane.

A recent photograph of The Burrs, c.1990.

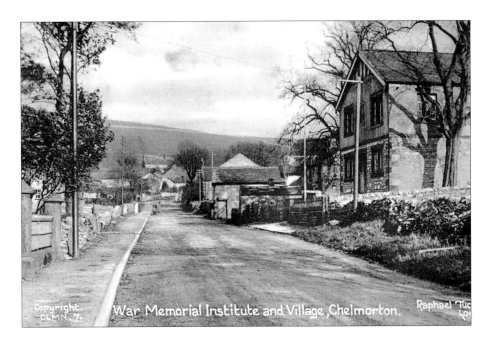

War Memorial Institute and Village, Chelmorton.

The Main Street, Chelmorton.

"You've not moved any wood yet?" "No", I said. *"Well, here's one step in the right direction. You know that top plantation?"* "Yes", I said. *"There's a small hen cote in it now, with five hens and a cockerel. Cote, hens and cockerel are yours if you want, so when you let them out and feed them in a morning, and when you shut them up at night, you can bring back a bundle of wood each time. Always try to do two jobs at once if you can."*

He must have taken advantage of the fog to move the cote into place without being seen from The Burrs - we would have been sure to have seen him normally. *"I've left the hens shut in after I moved the cote - so you can let them out yourself. When the hens come out into their new environment, you will be part of it."*

The next morning, when they'd had time to settle down, I went to let them out. I lifted up the small sliding hen hole door and fastened it up. I stood back and watched. Slowly, with a great deal of clucking, the cockerel appeared, closely followed by five large and beautiful hens. He stood still for a minute, in the small doorway, looking his new kingdom over - and he seemed to approve. I was in business on my own and I had not yet started school.

Pig on a motorbike

The hens did very well, laying large brown eggs. When in late spring they went broody, my Dad got some orange boxes with three compartments in each, which made good nests. He put a square of turf, with soft straw on top, in the bottom of each compartment and then, when we required them to brood, introduced the hens to their new nests. After inspection they always took to them and when they had been sitting on the nest for a day or two, we would place about twelve eggs (or as many as she could cover, according to her size) under each hen, letting her out once a day for food and water and to stretch her legs.

There was always great excitement when the chickens finally began to hatch because you can't count chickens before they hatch. You do not want more than one cockerel to twenty or thirty hens, so all the male chickens were sold for the table as soon as they were large enough. People wanted big chickens in those days so Mr Grindey's gift was blossoming out into a nice flock of poultry.

Mr Grindey had monitored my progress over two years and was pleased with what he saw, in fact so pleased that, one day, while I was collecting water, he showed me a litter of young pigs. Now, I had seen a lot of pigs belonging to my Grandad and had heard a lot of talk that his pigs were pedigrees, for showing at the big shows - and winning at most of them. So I had heard a lot of talk as to the shape and conformation of the best of pigs. Even at my tender age, I think I knew quite a lot about them.

"What do you think of this lot?" Mr. Grindey asked. *"Well, they are a nice even litter,"* I said. Then I stood there and spent some time picking out the best to my mind. He knew what I was doing. *"Well,"* he said, after a few minutes, *"Which is the best?"* I pointed out a young boar. *"That one,"* I exclaimed, with precocious authority. Then he said, *"Which is the best gilt?"* Without hesitation, I picked four out. *"It will be one of those four. To pick out the best would be very hard at this age. It will be easier in a month or two."*

"All right," he said, and he reached down, ready to mark the one nearest to me with black lead, *"She will be weaned one week on Saturday. I am giving her to you. You better go and get your Dad to make a pen ready."* I looked at him in disbelief. Was he giving me a little pig of my own? *"You've got a good level bunch, Mr Grindey,"* I said again, showing my embarrassment and disbelief.

The Hall, Dated 1634, Chelmorton.

The Village from South, Chelmorton.

"Thank you", he said, *" Yes, I am making you a present of one of them. Take your pick. Come on,"* he said, *"Which one do you want?"*

That really woke me up. Taking no notice of the one Mr Grindey was pointing out, I chose a strong female. *"That one,"* I said. With that he put a strong black lead mark across her shoulders.

Off I went home, but I said nothing to anyone till Dad got home from work. I think he had mixed feelings when I told him, because Grandad would not have any other pigs at the Burrs except pedigree ones when he was there. Anyhow, we made a warm draught-proof pen ready. Dad had by now bought Mr Chapman's old motorbike and sidecar. Saturday came at last and off we went on the motorbike to collect my pig, and when Dad saw which one I had picked, he was very pleased.

After thanking Mr Grindey sincerely, off we went home with the little pig in the sidecar. We put it into its nice clean pen but it was obviously lonely leaving its family, so I spent a lot of time talking to it and it soon began to chatter back. What it was saying I did not know, but after three or four days, it used to carry on when I left it. By now, I had called her Molly.

One warm day, I decided to let Molly out and she did not run off, but followed me like a pet dog. Now and again, she would give a kind of bark and tear round the yard two or three times, to let off steam. She now began to answer to her name. I did not have a dog - and now I did not need one. Everywhere I went, she went, collecting firewood, feeding my hens. When I went in the house for meals, she waited on the doorstep. That is, until one day Ma had baked some apples. The smell of those apples was too much for Molly, so in she came and plonked herself beside me. All was well until she sat up and her snout poked above the table. Ma saw it and we were both outside on the end of Ma's broom!

As the months passed, Molly grew and grew. It would soon be time for her to start a family of her own. She certainly would not fit into the sidecar any more, so other arrangements had to be made. We took the sidecar off the motorcycle and replaced it with a crate five feet six inches long and wide enough for her, and with two doors. We could then load her in through the rear door, so she could see where she was going and unload her through front door.

I had been training Molly to get in and out, by giving her titbits, first at the door and then further down the crate, until she would walk through it without problems. When it was time to take her to see a boar, we opened the rear door and in got Molly! The front door was closed and as soon as she had got through the rear door, we closed that one too. She shook her head in discontent for the first half mile, then seemed to settle down to enjoy the ride out. The few motorists that were knocking about in those days had not seen a pig going for a ride before, especially on a motorbike.

In due course, Molly had twelve of a litter - eight gilts and four boars - very good for a start. She was a very good mother, very proud of her little ones and she loved to have us talk to them and admire them. We sold four of the gilts and three boars, after weaning at eight weeks old. Grandad came and castrated the boar which we fed up for meat, bacon and ham.

Two weeks before Christmas the butcher arrived one night. Knowing the date of his visit, we had got the pig ready by only giving it a light feed on the two previous days so its stomach would be empty. We had two old wash boilers with good fires under them and full of boiling water. One of the empty pig cotes had been scrubbed out ready. The pig was stunned, then stuck with a sticking knife. As the blood poured out, it was caught in a clean bucket, and we stirred a handful of salt into the blood to stop it clotting. Then buckets of boiling water were poured over the pig and the bristles scraped off with a scraper.

When this hard work was done, the pig was hung up on a cambrel which had a rope attached to it. The rope went over a pulley fastened in the roof. When all was ready, two men pulled on the loose end of the rope, and one pulled the carcass up, back legs first. When it was up where it was wanted, the end of the rope was tied to a stout post, leaving the carcass hanging free. The butcher then dressed it, taking the insides out.

The liver and other organs were placed on big dishes to go into the house to be made up into savoury ducks and the blood for black puddings. The head would be cut up and boiled for a long time to make brawn. When the carcass had cooled and set, the next day it was let down onto a bench for cutting up into joints. The hams and bacon were put in salt on stone benches, salt being rubbed vigorously into the meat so it would keep for months. The leaf fat was taken into the house to be cut up into one inch pieces and then put into roasting tins which were put into the oven to render out all the lard. After all the fat had run off you were left with crisp scratchings. You cannot buy such lard today nor scratchings so crisp and tasty.

There are so many by-products of a pig. With having no refrigeration we gave some of the pork away - a prime cut each to Mr. Grindey, Joe Hallam, the insurance collector, Mr Chapman, Mr Phillips, who used to bring the groceries once a week, the postman and some relations.

Uncle Herbert with a prize pig at a show.

Sunday school and Christmas

When the weather was reasonable Muriel and I would go to Sunday school on Sunday mornings. Later on when Joyce was a little older, she also went. It was a very long walk for small children but some of our friends took my sisters to their houses for lunch, and kept them entertained until it was time for the afternoon service - while I walked home and came back again. Then after afternoon service we would all go home together.

We always had a Sunday School party at Christmas. After a big feed it was present giving time and the child with the most attendances got the first pick off the tree. I still have a Bible from one of those parties.

Chelmorton chapel

I remember one year when the nights had got longer and the days colder and things outside were *"rate miserable"*. But in the house a good log fire had changed all that. The animals had been fed and shut up comfortable for the night, there was enough fuel in and the water containers were full - one big bucket for washing faces, hands and pots, and a gallon jug for boiling to make drinks. Then it was shut the door and bolt it, put the bag along the bottom and draw the heavy, brown woollen curtain. across. Now wellies off, shoes or slippers on, a good wash and tea.

Mum and Dad started to talk of Christmas. What to have for dinner - one of the big cock chickens, or get Grandad to come and kill a pig? The table came first, any luxuries like asking me what I wanted Father Christmas to bring came later. I wanted a waggon to cart stuff about. We had a very large chimney, so I thought he could manage one all right, so long as he could get past the bar with the three linked chains and hooks hanging from it.

As the shortest day came, preparations were into full swing; baking, boiling, roasting, icing, decorating. Outside, we did all we could to make it possible to have as little to do on Christmas Day as necessary; cattle have got to be fed and looked after every day of the year. We always had a good supply of pine logs to burn at Christmas. All was set! Hang the stockings up, and leave the mince pie and glass of wine for Father Christmas.

At last Christmas morning arrived. By the time Ma allowed me to get up, Dad had done all his outside jobs for the day, feeding and watering the stock and just got back in. My stocking was full of goodies: nuts, an apple, an orange and a few sweets; some books and crayons. Then I saw it - under the table it stood - A RAILWAY ENGINE! - a green model of the real thing.

Probably the best toy I ever had, it was big enough to ride and the tender could be used to cart stone, gravel, sand and no end of stuff about. I could pull it along with a piece of string or sit on the boiler and push it along with my feet. When I got to where my load was needed, I could turn my engine round and back up, then lift the front, tipping out the load. I used it all day long for all kinds of handy jobs. Although my Dad only made it from spare pieces of wood found around the farmyard, it lasted me at least five years.

Stella and me.

Where there are farmers gathered

As hay-time approached, Mr Grindey asked Dad how he was going to get the meadows cut and the hay into the barn. Dad said Uncle Norman would come over from Grandad's with a pair of horses and a mowing machine and cut the grass, but we would have to do the remainder by hand. Then Mr Grindey said Dad could have Stella.

Stella was a brown mare, a bit lame but alright doing light work. But she was very crafty. If she knew there was work to do she was very lame until the job was done. Then when we let her out into the field afterwards, she would gallop round like a two-year old.

The only usable cart left at the Burrs was a large pig or sheep float which was no use for carting anything else and was in any case too heavy for Stella to pull. Its big wooden wheels with its iron tyres dug into the ground like all the other carts of those days. So we borrowed a light cart from Mr. Bagshaw and managed for that season. But Dad had a plan in his mind to build a much handier cart, closer to the ground, which would be much easier to load and cause less damage to the ground. To put this plan to the test, materials had to be found. Having no money to buy them, it was a case of making do with what there was around the place.

On the hayloft were some large boards, 12 feet by 10 inch planks one inch thick, which Grandad had bought some years before to fasten to the floors of the pig cote to make warm beds for the pigs to lie on. *"I don't know what your Grandad will say, but we will use four of them for the new cart,"* said Dad.

Next we needed shafts and several spars of good sound timber - preferably ash. Not having anything like this on the farm we turned our attention to the ironwork. In the corner of the yard was a scrap iron heap and from this, with a great deal of imagination, we managed to select enough for what was needed. That kept us busy for a long time. We had to cut and drill by hand to shape and bend the material and Dad used the house fire to get the iron hot, then he fashioned it, using a 56 lb weight as an anvil, and a chisel and a punch to cut holes. He got the front axle of an old Calino car, but had to buy new bead edged tyres for it. .

But we still needed the spars and shafts. Dad was working in Blackwell Mill Quarries at the time. A heading - a tunnel about 20 feet long - had been driven, with two more tunnels off it at right angles for 16 feet each. At the end of these two, chambers were hewn out about twelve feet square and eight feet high. When all this was done, the chambers were filled with gunpowder - up to ten tons in each chamber. Wires with detonators at the end were laid from the gunpowder to the outside ready to be connected to the charger wire. Lastly the tunnels were re-filled with rock and clay to seal the gunpowder in. All was ready for the big blast.

Who would have the pleasure of pressing the plunger which sent an electric charge through wires to the detonators to explode the gunpowder and move thousands of tons of rock in a split second? A member of the royal family was invited and accepted the honour, so a very large, strong viewing shelter was built, half a mile away for safety, yet having a first class view of the quarry face about to be blown out.

The great day came and wires were laid from the heading to the shelter. At the appointed time, a member of the royal family arrived to perform the pressing of the plunger. There was not a bang, but a great rumble. The ground shook for miles around and the whole rock face was lifted upwards and forwards, bringing thousands of tons of rock down ready to be broken into smaller pieces with 21 to 28-pound hammers. The men, who broke them into manageable sizes and then loaded them into two ton wagons, were paid at the rate of eight old pence (8d.) a ton. The wagons were taken on a narrow gauge track over a weighbridge, and then tipped into the kilns, where a layer of stone alternated with a layer of coal until it was full, and then, as the coal burnt for up to seven days, the stone became very, very hot until it changed into lime, ready for use in industry and agriculture.

After the dust had settled and all the dignitaries had gone, the shelter was taken down and cleared away except for one ash beam eighteen feet long and one foot by four inches square. How or why it was left, I don't know - I suppose it was probably too heavy to bother loading. But luck would have it that Dad used to walk to work that way, and after it had been lying there a few weeks, he decided to ask the works manager about it. At the time there was a very good manager, who tried to get round the quarry every day, speaking to everyone on his way round as he sought to make sure the rock face was safe for his men to work at.

Dad waited for his chance. One morning, the manager was not in a hurry when he stopped to speak to Dad. He asked him if all was well at work and at home. Dad said it was, thank you. *"By the way sir, you know when the shelter was removed from off Mr Spencer's ground, a lump of timber was left lying there and wants moving."* "*Oh,*" said the manager, "*How big is it?*" Dad told him. "*I will have it moved. It wouldn't be any use to you at all, Charles?*" "*.....Well, yes,*" Dad said. "*You can have it, if you can move it - and let Mr Spencer know I am sorry it has been left behind on his field. If he needs a load of lime or stone, I'll send him one for any inconvenience caused.*"

On Friday night, Dad asked me to go and see Mr Chapman the next day and ask him if he could bring his motorbike and side-box down to the Burrs as soon as he could. When I went to Chelmorton the next morning to collect meat from Mr Rains, the butcher, and other things from the grocers, Mr Chapman said he would come as soon as he had had his dinner. He arrived at one o'clock on a 1925 BSA SV, with its big side-box ,and with his son Tony riding on the pillion seat. Tony and I went off on some adventure or other, while Dad put a pair of plough lines in the side box and off they went.

After about an hour, they came back with their load. The side-box was five feet long so there were six foot six inches sticking out both front and rear. They unroped it and lifted the 18 foot ash beam onto two forty gallon oil drums Dad had left ready. The spars and shafts had duly arrived - but all in one lump.

.   While the work on the cart was in progress, our usual visitors took a keen interest as to what kind of folly would be created with the collection of timber, steel bolts and an axle. As the cart, the like of which had not been seen before, began to take shape, the comments were varied and often humourous. Then, suddenly, someone noticed it was five feet wide whereas the doorway of the barn was only four feet. No one said anything to us as the story spread round Chelmorton like wildfire.

As Easter approached, the cart only needed a few final touches before it was ready for painting. The local farmers were at a loss to know how we intended to get the cart out of the shed, and not wanting to ask themselves, they got some one to come down to the Burrs for a hair cut to find out for them. Ron Lindley was chosen - he used to have his hair cut by my Dad when we lived at Chelmorton. During this particular haircut which did not last long, he asked my Dad when we were going to launch the cart into the wide world. "*Oh,*" said Dad, "*Next Sunday is Easter Day, that will do.*" "*What time? I will give you a lift with it if you like,*" said Ron. "*10 o'clock will be as good a time as any,*" Dad replied. So off he went to report back to the assembled company at the Church Inn.

Sol Mellor at Nether Low.

Not wanting to miss a good laugh at our expense for making a cart too wide to get out through the doorway, locals began to arrive at the Burrs on Sunday morning to witness at first hand the performance. They had swallowed the bait, hook, line and sinker!

It was a lovely spring morning with the lapwing and curlew calling as they claimed their territory. They started arriving about 9.45. Mother had been baking fruit pies and cakes, together with tea by the mugful. It was to be a real family effort.

An old gypsy friend turned up with a light horse and dray. Two of his boys, each riding a half-wild pony, followed. *"Good morning Mush,"* he said, brightly to my Dad. *"Hello m'chavie"*, he said to me, in his rough friendly voice. *"Good morning, Tom"*, my Dad replied.

Now Tom had not come to make fun of someone's mistake. Tom knew that where there were farmers gathered, there would be money. He had come to do business, to sell the two ponies which looked so good and quiet while his boys were handling them. And on the dray were bundles of ware - clothes pegs made from hazel, carnations from elderberry, and cow sticks and walking sticks from ash plants.

Others were arriving from different directions, so at 10 o'clock Tom and Dad went into the stable to bring the cart out. Instead of wheeling it out, they removed the wheels and turned the cart over onto its side, on to three rollers. They trundled it neatly through the doorway, once outside turning it right way up again and putting the wheels back on, to the approval and applause of the gathered spectators.

Now if we had used Stella to demonstrate the cart, she may have put on one of her very lame acts, so while the wheels were being tightened, Tom took his horse out of his dray shafts and put it into the shafts of the new cart. Proudly he got into the cart and off he went like Ben Hur round the field several times. We had a heap of big stones at the bottom of the field at which he stopped and, with some willing help, put near enough one ton of stones into the cart, then walked at his horse's head and took the load round a wet two acre meadow, leaving no wheel marks, the light horse pulling its load with ease. This was the same load which, in the carts used by farmers at that time, would have left deep wheel marks where they cut into the ground and would have needed two heavy shires to pull them.

Before the demonstration was over, the cart was sold and there were firm orders for three similar ones. We were in business, for the cash for this one would buy

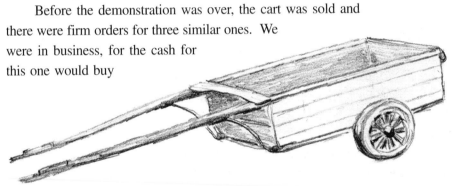

materials for others. As the locals headed back to Chelmorton, they realised that perhaps it was not all that foolish to make a cart in a building with the door too small. The idea of it had got them there to the demonstration and sold that cart and others.

So it was no accident that Tom arrived with his light horse - my Dad knew that gypsies' horses are tougher and stronger than they look and Tom was a first class horse and show man. A lot of people learned a lesson that day.

Tom and my Dad congratulated each other on the day's work. Dad said, *"You know Tom, you wouldn't do amiss to replace your dray wheels with two car axles with pneumatic, blown-up tyres. It'd make for easy rolling and quietness."* Tom replied, *"No, thank you, Mush; my horses' hooves talk to me and my wagon's wood and steel wheels sing to me. I wouldn't like to travel any other way"*.

Salford Coop visit to supplying farmers at Shepley, 1933.

How to read the book of nature

In the years that followed I spent as much time as I could with gypsy children when they were staying in the green lanes nearby. I learned their language and their ways - how to live off the land, the best places to survive when caught in a storm or if stranded without reaching shelter by night fall, and how to read the book of nature and the mind of animals. A genuine gypsy has knowledge beyond belief about the natural world, managing to live when you and I would starve.

I remember that while going along a narrow green lane some gypsy children were pointing out things to me which we could eat. So when we came to a hawthorn tree, I let them know that I also knew a bit about nature, saying *"You can eat the leaves off the thorn tree and bush."* *"Yes"*, said one them, called Joe after his Dad, *"now tell me how you make them good to eat"*. I did not know - all I knew was you could eat them, and I admitted this.

When we got back to where they were camping, there was a good smell of leek and hare soup coming from a large cast iron cooking pot hung over a wood fire, a steaming kettle at its edge. There were clean sheets hanging over thorn bushes to dry. They had been there for three or four days. As we wandered over to them, Joe picked two or three hawthorn leaves and started to chew them, telling me to do the same - but they were bitter so we both spat them out. Joe moved part of a  sheet. The leaves where it had been were much paler green. We took a few of the paler leaves and to my amazement they were quite good to eat. *"You do the same with dandelions and many other things,"* Joe laughed.

Later in my life, while in the army attending lectures on survival, if the young officer in charge of the lecture was boring or snobbish, I would wait my chance and, like Joe, I would ask the question about how can such a diet be made palatable. On one occasion the lecturer, with the Company Sergeant-Major looking on, tried to have his own back on me, for he thought he was an expert on shelter. He asked me to point out how I would find the best shelter for the night out in the field, using a map and taking into consideration the wind direction and other factors. He was expecting me to read the map for contours and make a fool of myself.

But unbeknown to him, I had been a civilian guide for the mountain rescue because of my local knowledge of safe sheep paths on the high moors, especially in dense fog or low cloud. The class waited for my reply. I was short and sharp. *"Ask the sheep, Sir."* *"Are you suggesting that sheep are wiser than I am?"* he exploded. *"Well, Sir"*, I said, in the broadest high peak dialect I could muster, *"Two yeds are better than one, even if it's only sheep; they find shelter every night. As you said, Sir - practice makes perfect, Sir."*

At this the CSM turned and walked out, looking at the ceiling and whistling a nondescript tune. Whether I should or should not have carried on in this way, I do not know. But the fact is there; watch the animals, they can tell you a lot, from where troops are concealed to when to expect a blizzard. Since then WO2 Wootton and I have been the best of friends! So perhaps I was right in pointing out the value of making use of nature when needed.

At half past three we were free to go from school

I had eventually started school four months before I was seven. Living on an isolated farm, no one had bothered much before then. It was just one mile across the fields and lanes. All the lanes in those days had three ruts; one worn by each wheel and one worn deep by the horses.

I never mastered writing but I learnt to read reasonably enough. Maths was all right but I really took to history, geography and the Old Testament. I remember a visit by the School Inspectors. I quite stunned them by claiming that the Devil worked for God. The Vicar with them said that indeed he did not. I replied by quoting the book and verses where it said that the Lord sent the Devil to tempt some one, so if He sent the Devil, the Devil must work for God. This argument went on for half on hour, finishing when they changed to the New Testament of which I knew nothing - I was not interested in what I could not understand.

We were taken to the museum at Buxton where I was very impressed to be shown a map of Roman settlements in Britain which featured the Burrs. Soon after this visit I started collecting historical artefacts from Palaeolithic, Neolithic, Bronze Age and Roman times. I soon realised that I was living in an area rich in such things.

The school itself was the same outside as it is today, some 60 years later, but inside there were coal fires on which water was boiled in large kettles to make a hot drink to have with sandwiches at dinner, as it was too far to go home. I used to take a mixture of cocoa and sugar in a small tin for the teacher to make me a hot cocoa drink.

The first lesson in the morning was scripture, and Miss Makinson read from the Old Testament. I liked to comment on what the Bible said after she had finished reading. Next came arithmetic. For this we all went into our own classes. I was still in Miss Mcevitt's class. This lasted for one hour, and was divided into a period chanting tables, then sums. But best of all for me was mental arithmetic - I would have the answers as fast as the teacher could read the questions.

At 10.45 we had a fifteen-minute break. In winter we would often make slides in the schoolyard on the ice. After break, it was what I dreaded - English. I could not spell at all and so I was always in trouble. It was horrible being made to stand or kneel in a corner, sometimes being whacked hard with a ruler. I still could not write my name when I got married.

At about 11.45, the big kettles were put on the fire to boil ready to make drinks for the teachers and the children from far off farms who stayed at school for dinner. We had one hour for dinner starting with the roll call.

On Friday afternoons we had geography, history or nature, then P.T. if it was fit to go out, if not, handicraft, papier-mâché or acting. The last period was singing - songs such as *Oh No John, The Ash Grove, In the Trees the Birds are Singing*. And at half past three, we were free to go.

On the way home, I had to go to Mr Grindey's for half a gallon of drinking water which I carried to the Burrs in an aluminium can with a lid and handle. After half a mile or so, I can tell you, it felt very heavy. Going towards Chelmorton along Common Lane, the farm was on the right hand side, opposite the old school. The last pasture before the farmyard had a round plantation in the middle of it, only a small one, maybe ten yards across, with a good dry stone wall all the way round about four feet high. It was very pleasing to look at but that was not the main reason for its siting in the middle of the field. It was there to give shelter to the cattle. With being round, no matter where the wind came from, one side always gave shelter from the storms in winter or the sun in summer. The farm was home to a mixed lot of animals: two horses, some milk cows with followers, sheep, pigs and poultry.

One afternoon, while filling my drinking water, I heard familiar sounds coming from the pig cote. Listening, I realised that the sow was giving birth to young ones. I went to the house door and knocked for someone to come. Mrs Grindey came, hands covered in flour; obviously she was baking. I asked if Mr Grindey was about because of what I had heard going on in the pig cote. She thanked me and disappeared into the house.

Out he came. He thanked me, then walked quietly to the pig cote door and listened, carefully opened it a little - just wide enough to see inside. He softly closed the door and came across to where I was waiting for him. *"She is getting on with her job,"* he said, in a low voice, *"So I'll leave her to it."* With that, I got off home to get my hens shut up before Foxy did his rounds. Make no

mistake: if a fox gets into a cote of hens, it will only take one, but it will bite the heads off the lot, no matter how many there are.

As soon as I got home, it was time to get changed into old working clothes and to go and feed the hens, collecting the eggs at the same time. When I got back from these jobs, Ma would have a hot drink and snack waiting. On Friday which was baking day, the snack would be a scone or a small cake of some kind.

Meadow Place, Chelmorton.

This is by Town End
before the council houses
were built.

Now it came to pass

The Burrs was a bit primitive. No electric, no water, no phone or gas. We had a paraffin lamp in the house and a storm lamp for outside - and candles. I had a candle in a jam jar with a piece of string tied round the top to carry it with. The toilet was dry and 50 yards from the house.

We kept a boar and the boar cote was next to the toilet. One day a pig from a neighbouring farm felt the need of a male companion. Not being able to get through the door to him, it looked for another way in. The small door on the back of the toilet, used to empty and cart away the night soil, was weak and Mrs Pig broke her way in but still found, between her and the boar, a solid wall. She tried to get out but only got hopelessly stuck in the small passage, which was two feet square and six feet long, with stonewalls on three sides. There was a wooden seat above her with two large holes in it and it had a flag floor.

Now, it came to pass that Ma, not knowing that there was a strange pig around, went to the toilet and got sat on the seat quite comfortably. The pig, had kept quiet, but now with a protesting roar made a fresh effort to get free, the bristles on the pig's back coming into contact with Ma's softer backside. She screamed and bolted out of the door, not having any idea at that moment what kind of a wild creature was under the seat.

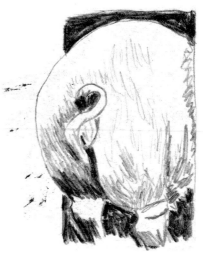

When she had eventually calmed herself, whatever it was, she decided, would have to remain there and not have any contact with the world outside. She ran into the house, reached a double-barrelled 12-bore shotgun off a beam, grabbed a handful of cartridges and ran out again, loading both barrels as she went. Carefully looking into the toilet again, she could see nothing. So she cautiously went round to the back and now saw that the small door was broken and realised there was a pig fast under the seat - and no danger to anyone. I was sent straightaway to the village to enquire as to whose pig it was so they would come for it.

I reluctantly set off for Chelly to make inquiries, and to try and find out who, if anyone had lost a pig. As I came to the end of Common Lane, turning right down the village, I had to pass the blacksmith's on my right and I could see a horse being shod while two or three more awaited their turn. One or two farmers, whose horses had been shod already, were standing talking, all of a heap. I decided it was best to ignore them and carried on to Wheeldon's butcher's shop, where George Wheeldon turned to me. *"What can I get for you, young man?"* I explained that I only wanted to know if he had heard of anybody who had lost a pig. *"Why should I hear of stray pigs?"* he said, rubbing his hands together, *"Go to the blacksmith's, see what they know there."*

So I plucked up courage and went back up the village to face the inquisition from the crowd that was congregated around George Smith, the blacksmith. I faced up to them and asked if any of them had lost a pig as one had turned up at the Burrs. There was silence for what seemed to be a long time. Then Jack Gould said, *"An extra pig at the Burrs will not make much difference amongst your lot. What's so different about this pig for you to come all the way up here?"* Then I put my foot in it, so to speak. *"This one's got fast under the lavatory and Ma did not know and upset it by sitting on it."* Well, a roar of laughter went up which they must have heard at Longnor. Then, all the horses and riders disappeared for home to spread the news.

When the owner finally turned up for the pig, they could not move her at first and, during this time she either suffocated in the night soil or died of a heart attack. With the pig being dead, the task of getting her out was at least easier. At last we had got our toilet back. Mum was not at all happy about the incident, and the boar was rehoused in one of a row of pig cotes at the other side of the yard so the same fiasco would not be repeated.

The same boar became very nasty and dangerous as he got older, being a good registered pedigree Large White. My

Dad tried to persevere with him but he became impossibly mad so Grandfather was sent for. Being the owner, it was his decision what to do. He opened the top door of the boar's cote a little to see him, when the boar charged him but the stout bottom door held. Seeing what he was like for himself, Grandfather said, *"Send for Redferns."* So the knacker dealers were sent for.

Eventually, a horse and special cart with high sides, and a hand winch for pulling casualties into it, arrived. Mr Redfern climbed down from the cart and inquired where the boar was. Assessing the situation, he got a 12-bore out of a box on the cart and said, *"Can you let the boar out?"* The door had a mechanical device so it could be opened and closed from the safety of the next pig cote. The door was opened. Mr Redfern was standing 25 yards away. The boar came slowly outside but seeing Mr. Redfern it turned into a ball of hate, muscle and fangs, and charged for him. Mr Redfern with one arm, one gun and one chance, calmly fired one barrel of his 12 bore. The pig stopped in its tracks for a second and then careered on towards him. He did not fire his second barrel as we all expected him to do. When the pig was just three yards away from him, it collapsed stone dead.

As he was taking the loaded and empty cartridges out and was blowing the soot and smoke from the used barrel, my grandad asked him why he had not used the second shot. He smiled dryly, *"No good wasting good ammo. When the pig stopped for a second after I fired, I knew he was dead. It was only momentum that brought him on."*

Uncle Herbert with another fine prize winner

Great Grandma,
Ann Sigley.

Grandad at Edale.

Once hired, you could not go back on it

Grandad stayed for a week or two and he used to talk to me for hours about the old days when he was young.

The pay for his first year's farm work, on a farm in Foxt, was 2/6d (30 old pence - 12.5p in today's money). Just think about it, 1p for a month's hard labour; six fourteen hour days a week, ten hours on a Sunday; two days off at Christmas. He was fed enough to keep him fit for work, and had only one pair of boots and trousers. For anything else to wear he had to rely on handouts. The do-gooders at the time were condemning slavery abroad while practising it at home.

When he went home that Christmas, the first thing he said to his Grandma was, *"Thank heavens I have finished working for that old hound."* *"Hey, Lad"* his Grandma said, *"He came to see me yesterday and I hired you out for another year. I took five shillings for another year. I didn't know you were so unhappy there. That's why he came yesterday before you could tell me yourself what you wanted to do."* In those days, once hired, you could not go back on it.

So Grandad had to work on for another year in those terrible conditions, starting at 4.00 am. If he was not dressed and out by 4.05 am, the old villain would rush into the attic where Grandad slept, grab his clothes, open the window and throw them out into the farmyard, regardless of the weather and mud outside. Grandad, who was only ten, would have to go out, find his clothes, put them on outside and then work in them, whatever the weather, wet, muddy or still dry. And he had to put up with many a beating when his boss was in a foul mood.

At long last, the second year was coming to an end. During late November and December, his boss became more civilised and pleasant to him. He was after Grandad for another year. In the last week of the year he went out to see Grandma to hire him for a third twelve-month period. But when he came back, he was back to his old self, a tyrant slave driver. She had turned on him, telling him he was not fit to have dog, never mind a boy, under his domination. My Grandad's father had died 5 years earlier, and his mother 12 months later, so there was no one to stand up for my Grandad except his grandmother.

When the time was up and Grandfather was going out of the farmyard, he turned to his boss and said, setting him with his large dark brown eyes, *"I will be back; maybe two, three, four, five or even six years. I will be back for what you have done to me and others before me. You will pay dearly when I am older and stronger; as sure as night follows day, I will be back."*

In the following years, he did various jobs, becoming a very good cyclist, winning many national races, especially in the hills. We still have many of his trophies. He was a good cricketer as well. But the old villain was never far from his mind. Six years or so later, as he had promised, he set off to settle the old score early one Sunday morning.

He was now living about thirty miles from Foxt. Arriving in the village about midday, he met someone he knew and got off his bike to have a few words. Then he saw an old farmer-friend further up the village, and he joined him. *"Good morning, John, and where are you going?"* asked the farmer, knowing full well where Grandad was going and why. *"I am going to settle with that old villain."*

"Eh, John, tha mus'na you know. You are a fit strong young man, and he's but an old man going childish. Ever since you left him, he has never been

My Grandad Fearns, c 1890s.

outside his own yard. As the years have gone by he has got frightened of his own shadow. He'll never answer the door after dark and he hires a man instead of young lads to protect him. If you go to settle now, you could be in deep trouble - and he will be free from the fear which has a grip on him. I don't know what you said to him, but it haunts him day and night. It is paying him back, sure enough."

He took Grandad into the farm house where Sunday dinner was ready. The farmer's wife, seeing him outside, had set a place at the table for him. After his meal, Grandad thanked his farmer friends for both the dinner and the advice, and now clear in his mind with a job well done, he left the old villain to live with his fear.

A sock too far

Having got a little money together, Ma wanted a sewing machine, so she saw someone in Buxton about buying one, and a demonstration was arranged.

Now there are two ways down to the Burrs, one down two fields off Caxterway and another down a very rough narrow lane, through one gate, down one field and into another rougher lane still, through another gate and across the little meadow. The sewing machine sales man chose the latter way, with the machines sliding all over his old car.

After she had seen one or two machines working, Ma bought a Singer and that was that, or so we thought! But the salesman noticed we had some very good cock chickens running about the farm. In fact, my Dad gave the salesman one of these for all the trouble he had taken to make sure Ma had the right machine.

Getting back to town, m'laddo told one of his Jewish friends about where he had been and the quality of chickens we had. Two days later, the Jewish gentleman arrived at the Burrs - taking good care to leave his car on the road, and walked down to the farm. He came into the house and was soon given a drink and a piece of cake. He talked to us about everything except the chickens.

Eventually we went outside to discuss the price of the chickens. Dad mentioned the price he wanted, and our new friend looked them over agreeing they were among the best he had ever seen and that Dad was not asking too much for them. But he explained he could not afford them all and so the sale could not be made. Not wanting to go back empty-handed, he said, *"I will pay your price for ten of them - any ten, you pick them out."* So my Dad agreed.

A week later, he was back for another ten, paying a little extra for the food they had eaten, and he kept coming till he had them all. Then he bought others as they became big enough for sale, and gradually he became a very good friend.

He was fascinating to listen to. He had come with his family from Russia to land in England, penniless but free. But he had met much resentment in this country in certain places. In one incident in Tideswell, one of his fellow refugees was going from house to house trying to sell clothing. Socks were his cheapest line and, seeing a young man sitting on an open windowsill, he called out, *"Socks, good and cheap socks"*, whereupon other young men appeared at

Tideswell church.

the window. One of them said, *"Come up here and we will give you socks"*. Not wanting to miss a sale of any kind he took his bag into the out-building of the Blue Bell Inn. Up the stairs he went, to find himself in the local amateur boxing ring. With the door closed behind him, he put his bags down and tried to talk his way out of the situation, but they meant to have him for sparring practice so he agreed to have some gloves fitted.

He stood with his arms by his side in the middle of the floor, there wasn't a proper ring. The best man among them had gloves on and began to take advantage, to the encouragement of the others, of the mug in the middle of the floor. After being hit far too hard for just sparring, the mug decided to come to life, taking up the style of the professional boxer he was. He pushed the bigheaded bully into some proper boxing now. Seeing their friend getting the worst of it - just what he deserved - the others foolishly joined in. Thirty seconds later, they were either knocked out or they had run out.

Things were more peaceful now, and the so-called mug took off his gloves and said to those that gathered around, *"I have taught you some manners, now learn to box. One of you may go far - anyone want to buy some socks?"*

By the next time he visited Tideswell everyone knew of him, and he was treated with respect, and had no trouble in selling to customers who wanted his wares. I am sure someone in Tideswell must remember him and the lesson of the Blue Bell Inn?

On one of our Jewish friend's visits he brought me an old book on farming. There was a lot about old breeds of cattle. He asked if I liked old books and I told him I liked the Old Testament. A surprised look came over his face and we talked about it for ages, in fact until it was going dark and it was time for me to go to bed.

I was beginning to discover the common humanity that all races share, and that all cultures have something different to offer, once you get to know them.

Tideswell

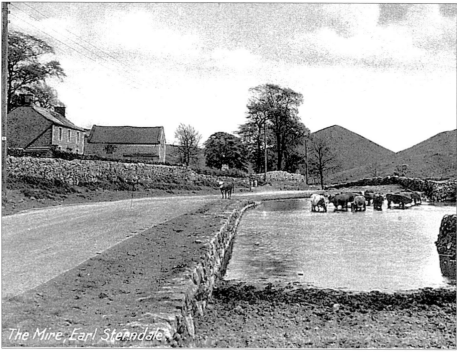

The Mire, Earl Sterndale

Poverty Cart

I then had two sisters, Muriel and Joyce. One occasion I remember is going with Ma and them to meet Auntie from off the Matlock bus at the RAC box on the A6 near Blackwell in about 1936. It was a two and a half mile walk each way. Ma had Joyce in a big pram with Muriel riding on the front. Just before we got to the bus stop, a front wheel came off - the split pin holding the wheel on had worn away.

After five minutes, the bus arrived. Auntie unloaded herself and some baggage and then came and gave each of us a big, horrible, sloppy kiss. I hated that and I have felt sorry for children having to put up with silly grown-ups forcing kisses on them ever since. Auntie took one look at the broken-down pram or 'poverty cart' as we called them and marched off towards a car parked near the RAC box. She borrowed the RAC key, unlocked the box and phoned for help. She must have used the car's number from which she had borrowed the key.

In less than twenty minutes, an RAC motorcycle and sidebox arrived - far more efficiently than today. As the RAC man alighted from his contraption, Auntie grabbed him, telling him how efficient and quick he was in answering her call as she lead him over to the perambulator. Between the praise and his embarrassment, he could not get out of making an effort at first-aid on the pram.

So he got out a piece of wire, cut it down to the right length and fitted it where the split pin had been. Auntie kept repeating what a nice man he was, what a very, very nice man. The pram was fixed, not quite as good as new, and off to the Burrs we went.

Of mice and moles and the National Park

In spring I set out to catch moles. Now Mr Mole is a cunning fellow. If you do not set the traps in the right run, in the right way, and if you leave the smell of human hands on the trap, he will fill your trap with soil and let it off. To catch a mole, look at the direction of the older heaps of soil compared to the newest. He's going that way!

Now using a half-inch by three foot round bar with a handle at one end, and sharpened at the other, press the bar into the ground at one inch intervals across the path of molehills. When you strike a run, the bar suddenly goes down into the ground very easily for an inch or so, then hard again as you go on past the run or tunnel. Next, take a small spade and dig a six-inch square hole down to the run, being careful not to touch the soil with your hands - use a stick specially cut for the job. Check where the run is and its direction, then place your trap so the mole will try to go through it, cover the hole you have made so no light can get down and then go away. Check your traps once a day removing any moles, then count and re-set your traps.

If you do not control the numbers of moles, they will turn a meadow into a ploughed field in twelve months, making it impossible to mow for hay.

Mouse catching was also a hobby of mine. A method I used was to fill a corn bin full of bran. Now mice love bran - they will find a way into the bin, feed on it and jump out as the bran is taken out to feed the cattle. It gets harder for them to get out, but they still jump in. Then you take extra out. If you gauged it right, next time they jumped in, they could not get out after feeding. Then I could catch them with my bare hands.

For some reason, Dr Smith came to visit us one day. I told him how I caught mice. He didn't believe that I could catch wild mice so I went to the corn store, caught a big mouse and took it into the house to show him. He took the mouse, thinking it was a tame one, put it on his knee and started to stroke it. To begin with, the mouse was stiff with fear but it soon got over its fear, bit his finger and bolted under some furniture. Lesson learned! The Doctor believed me after that.

On another occasion when he came to the house, my Dad had a high performance AJS motorcycle which he had taken to pieces and reassembled, but he couldn't get the timing right. The Doctor was very interested in engines, so he took off his jacket, rolled up his sleeves and set to work on the motorbike engine. After half an hour and getting covered all over with oil, the engine was perfect. Then he got covered in mud riding it all round the fields!

My Dad would never normally ride around the herb and flower rich fields at all because of the damage it could and would do to the fields, never mind the noise. You see, long before the National Parks were set up costing the taxpayers millions of pounds, the farmers were proud of their grassland, gates and dry stone walls and kept them neat and tidy. There were competitions between them, even in skills such as building and thatching hay or corn stacks, for farmers have always been conscientious, highly skilled and underpaid servants of the land. As my Grandad always said, *"Although we own the land we have only got it on trust and we should leave it better than we found it for the next generation."*

Haymaking at Hollinsclough in the 1930s.

Roadmending. Mr Bagshaw is on the left holding the horse.

A fine picture of the Rogers family in the 1930s.

Water was scarce

Dad had an old motorbike he never used, so one day I decided to get it going. After playing around with it for some time I found there was no petrol in the tank. With no petrol available, I decided to fill it up with water thinking it would go. Dad was very annoyed, mainly because he realised that if I had found the two gallon petrol can and spilled it filling the tank, then tried to start it, a spark could have had disastrous results. But all I got was a severe telling off.

It wasn't as bad as the time I refused to get a proper wash in the cold weather. There was so much ice on the kitchen window that you couldn't see through it. I only had a drop of warm water that I had carried from the boiler at the side of the fire in the house, so I had only wet my face and gone back to use the towel. Dad caught me at it and sent me back to wash again. Protesting loudly, I went back into the kitchen but by now the water had been tipped out of the enamel bowl we used for washing, so I needed more. Hot water was very scarce, so I only did the same again. I wet my face, made a dash for the clean towel and wiped myself dry.

It was then that Dad noticed the now black towel. He picked up a bucket, a scrubbing brush and soap, grabbed me, and outside to the mere we went. After breaking the ice on the pond, he filled the bucket with cold water went back into the yard, put the bucket of water down on a stone bench, made me strip to the waist and gave me a good scrubbing. Although it was freezing, it all happened too fast to get really cold. In fact, after I was dry and dressed, I felt really warm!

As I told new recruits in the army years later, the coldest part of washing in cold water is thinking about it. Many of the other sergeants who were used to the comfort of the Sergeants' Mess did not agree with me.

Lincoln Longwool Hoggs owned by Sam Swindell.

Mr Rogers and his son in the 1930s.

Feathers, blood and boot blacks

On the day of the Royal Jubilee in 1935, the village put on a great party for all the children, giving us a Jubilee mug each, and at night huge beacons were lit on certain hills in the distance. We had one on Chelmorton Low. I was too young to go to it but could see it plainly from the Burrs.

In the same year Mrs Pickford came to look after us while Ma was in hospital. She went in on the Friday and on Saturday morning, before he went to work, Dad told Mrs Pickford there was a chicken to cook for dinner in the coalhouse (not saying which one or where). After breakfast we looked for the chicken, but we could not find it, but I soon caught another for her. While I held the chicken by its legs, Mrs P got an empty dolly tub for the feathers and then she took the chicken from me and tried to pull out the chicken's neck. Being a large cock chicken, she could not manage it, but, not to be beaten, she took it over to the chopping block. Taking up the axe, she held the chicken so that its neck was across the block and swung the axe.

The now headless cock chicken flapped its wings and, with blood pouring from its severed neck, it flew everywhere. Eventually it stopped, and now, holding it over the dolly tub she plucked out all the feathers, dressed it and put it in the oven.

When Dad got home about 12.30 pm he saw the feathers and blood and asked, *"What's been going on?"* Mrs P told him of the drama and Dad laughed *"There's another one hung up behind the coal house door, you had better cook that for tomorrow"*. It did not worry Mrs P. She was a large jolly lady, always smiling. I think Mr Pickford had been killed in the 1914-1918 war.

A lot of men from the villages and farms worked on the quarries. My Dad worked at various quarries, starting at Topley Pike with Grandad, then at Grin. After he got married, he worked in the kilns, where he said the conditions were terrible. From there he went to Hill Head, to Hindlow, to Brierlow, then finally to Blackwell Mill where the best conditions existed, although he said two of the others were good.

But Blackwell Mill was nearby and he was pleased when he managed to get a job there. He mainly did filling up, that is breaking large stones down to whatever size was needed, twelve inch for the kilns and seven inch for Brunner Mons Chemicals over in Cheshire (later ICI).

The chargehand or foreman kept an eye on the size being filled. To help them do this they had a piece of steel, the shape of a tennis racket with a seven-inch hole in it. If they picked a stone out of the truck that would not fit through the hole, the truck was tipped over and the lot had to be reloaded. This had to be done to stop large stones reaching the customer, because if this happened, the customer would make the quarry fetch the lot back - maybe hundreds of tons.

If a horseman was on holiday or off sick, my Dad went on his job. My Dad liked handling the horses on the quarry but the pay was less than filling up, so he could not afford to do it regularly. The horses were stabled at a local farm run by the Wains at Wormhill Meadow. It was a steep meandering climb up from the river, under the railway and up to the meadow after a hard day's work. It had once been a carriage way, but is now only used by horses and motor cycles - I went up and down it with both horses and car over forty years ago and so long as the Wormhill Parish Council does not allow it to be downgraded to a footpath, you can use it yet.

Dad and some of his friends from the quarries had been saving up to go on a trip to London, but when it came time to go Ma was still in hospital, so Dad could not go. They were leaving the Quarry at 7.00am, by coach to Miller's Dale Station to catch the Manchester to London express. The men got to the quarry at about 6.30 am and they started to wonder what to do about Dad's money - with not being able to go, he ought to have some back.

It would be much better if someone else could go in his place, it was voiced. Dad had been hoping Ma would have been out of hospital in time for the trip so he had left it too late to try to get anyone to take his place. One work man, who was not going, said that, if he had known, he would have gone. His mates seized on the idea but he protested that he had no suitable clothes with him. No problem they said, so with a lot of swapping and borrowing, he was geared up except for shoes - it was too late to do anything about that, *"Keep your quarry boots on and you can get a boot black to black and polish them for a tanner"*. With that, off they all went to Millers Dale station and on to the London Express.

The clay-covered boots were getting some queer looks from some of the city type travellers. When the train stopped at St Pancras, folk were like sheep-going everywhere and getting nowhere, or so it seemed, and, as the little party of revellers set off for the exit, one was walking ahead to look for a shoeblack. Seeing one he dashed over to book the man's services for his friend. The man with the offending boots approached the shoeblack, who gave him a nod, *"Put your right foot on here,"* he said, pointing to his box and he started work on the boot. He spent ten minutes on that boot cleaning and polishing it, *'till you could see your face in it'*. *"Will that do?"* he said. *"It will that, it's grand,"* replied the quarry man. With that the shoe man grabbed his gear up and went off, leaving him with one clay-covered boot and one highly polished. There was not another shoeblack to be found anywhere in London! He had to go round London like that all day and all the way home.

He never knew that his mate who had found the shoe-black had given him 2/6d extra to clean only one boot, and another of the quarry men was up in front tipping shoe blacks to keep out of sight while the party went past.

Harvesting the Croft End fields at Chelmorton.

Balancing act

I learned to ride a bike in those days on grass. First an old bike frame with handlebars, then two sound old pram wheels - so a low bike. Push the contraption up the field so it can free-wheel down. Then get on, set off, fall off, get on, fall off - all the time into the soft grass, so no harm done. After sticking at it for a day, I mastered the art of balancing a bike. After this I used to go to the top of the field and take off - only ten mile an hour, I suppose, but it was like flying to me.

When Dad got the chance, he built me a proper bike out of two or three scrap ones he had picked up. Now I could get to the village and back in half an hour. One morning I set off to go to Cowdale to spend the day with my cousin George. There was a crosswind blowing as I made my way along the A515 between Brierlow Bar and Heathfield Nook. About halfway there, the extra pressure from a very big box wagon passing me, blew me onto the grass, I fell off the bike and ended up under the wall. As I collected myself and the bike up, I saw the big wagon disappearing into the distance. I said to myself there and then, and to any neighbouring cows that could hear me, that I would have one of those wagons myself when I grew up. In fact, the very first time in my life I drove a vehicle, it was a wagon.

My Uncle Mo was bailiff for Mr Morton at Cowdale. They used a motor wagon on the farm when carting hay. George, then twelve years old, used to drive it from row to row of heaped hay while the men loaded the hay onto it. In one flat field he taught me how to drive while the men were loading. I was ten years old. In later years, serving with the Royal Electrical Mechanical Engineers (R.E.M.E.), I was a Class I vehicle and recovery mechanic, so I had to drive all manner of vehicles, from jeeps to tank transporters. Even now, after driving 30 ton-plus juggernauts, I still remember that little lad being blown off his bike, especially when passing cyclists. H.G.V. drivers take notice - give them plenty of room.

One of my juggernauts.

Nowadays my daughter, Sarah, also holds an H.G.V. Class I licence.

The art of ambush

To supplement what we could grow, Dad had a 4.10-folding shotgun to go hunting for meat - rabbit, hare, partridge, pheasant, grouse, wild duck, moorhen or goose - anything edible in fact. To balance this with nature, he also tried to keep the number of foxes, stoats and weasels down.

My first gun was a Diana air rifle. I only ever took one rabbit but I learned the art of hunting; to take advantage of the wind, the full moon and the weather; to be able to walk without a sound or more important any vibration, to which animals are very sensitive; to walk on the ball of my feet first and not on the heels, for when walking one's heel causes vibrations which travel through the ground; how to take full  advantage of cover such as bushes, trees, rocks, walls, contours, taller grasses and other plants. In short, I learnt the Art of Ambush

I learnt that animals usually feed with their backs to the wind for maximum protection. They can hear and smell what is behind them in the wind and see any movement in front. I learnt the truth of the old saying, *"It always comes to him who waits in the right place at the right time"*. This is quite true, indeed gypsies can catch all they need without a gun.

Years later I had a group of young soldiers sent to me while on exercise in the Black Forest. It was blackest dark under the pine trees at night and they were afraid of doing night guard duty, so I got them together, then sat on a mound with my back to the forest. *"Now"* I said *"You do not have to be able to see, to know where your enemy is. Use your ears at all times."* I stayed where I was, with my back to the forest and told two of them to go round in a big half circle and try to creep up behind me. If they could get within twenty paces of me undetected, they would not have to do guard duty for a month.

As soon as they had set off, I got the remainder in a row either side of me, with their backs to the forest like me. When they were seated I told them not to look behind but if they heard anything at all, put their right arm straight out in front of them - not upwards, as the men creeping up behind would see it.

After about half an hour, two of the sitting group suddenly put their arms out. We stayed as we were, keeping calm and still. Then another two minutes passed and another arm went out, then another and another until all were out in front of them. *"Advancing soldier, stand still"* I commanded, without turning round. One of them moved, *"Stand still, that man to my left"*. He must have thought I had eyes in the back of my head. *"Right, you lot; in the sand in front of you, at the side of the road, write with your finger how many paces each of the advancing men are away."* I wrote what I thought on the paper on my clipboard, and asked each of them in turn what sand writings they had done. *"Five yards, sir,"* *"Four yards, sir"*, *"Ten yards, sir"*. This last was the furthest estimate I got.

"Right, get up, turn round and see where they are." *"But they are at least forty paces away, Sir"*, they all said at once. The first one to put his arm out said, *"I thought they were nearer than that when I first heard them"*. *"You did not hear them,"* I replied *"that is why I said 'As you were'"*. *"What did I hear then, Sir?"*

"You heard a rabbit bolting out of their way and the reason you heard it was because it crashed through the undergrowth making as much noise as it could to warn other animals who may not have seen them. That rabbit told me they were coming and from which direction. As I said, it does not matter whether you can see or not, you must listen - then very few people can get near you. If you are on duty yourself, do not make any noise but listen to others. If you do have someone getting close to you, it is because he marked the spot where you were, just before dark, and waited. One of the best things to do is to make some noise like blow your nose, cough or clear your throat to make him sure  *of where you are. Then move a few paces away to the left or right, very silently. Wait till he has gone past you. Then challenge from the rear. You must not be afraid of the dark. It can be a good friend if you make use of it by listening."*

On an exercise in the Black Forest, we had got the workshops set up in the centre, with the RASC in defensive position round the rear and infantry outside. We should have been fairly safe from attack by the 'Phantasians' - as the supposed enemy were called. After we had been in this position for two days, two soldiers came about mid-day wanting spares. Nothing odd about that but these two were looking around too much and left in the opposite direction from which they had come, taking stock as they went. My suspicion was aroused. Nothing happened until 1.00 am, when a vixen cried out about 200 yards away, then another about 100yards to the left of the first. Then a covey of partridges got up, further to the left again and the first vixen cried out again.

"That's no fox", I said to myself, and went and found the captain. *"We've got visitors coming up on us Sir"*. *"Are you sure?"* *"Yes sir."* *"Call stand to,"* he said. *"What about the forward gun crew? They will not know what is happening until it is too late. Give me five minutes to get them closer in before stand to. I've alerted some already but if we call stand to, the balloon will go up"*. He gave me five minutes to move the machine gun crew. I moved swiftly but silently to the gun pit, whispering to them to keep dead silent, bring their weapons and follow me.

We had got half way back to the main position when stand to was called. Ten seconds later a thunder flash was thrown into the now empty gun pit. We had just made cover near the main defences when flares lit up the whole area showing up the attackers in front of us. With no cover, how many blank rounds were fired in the next three minutes, I would not like to guess. The umpire's decision was that the Phantasians were completely outwitted and wiped out.

In the debrief, the officer in charge of the attack asked what had alerted the REME, who were thought to be a soft target, to their presence, when they had successfully got through the infantry and the RASC undetected. *"Your pair of foxes did not call to each other in English"*, the REME captain said, *"The two advanced platoons gave the fox cry to let each other know where they were, while creeping up, first on the forward machine gun pit to put it out of action and then on the main attack force to hit and take the workshop area. It was bad luck for them there was someone in REME who understood the language of the fox!"*

Next time you go to the country for the day, be careful of the thick-looking old farmers, you do not know what they actually know or where or what they have been in the past. In fact, if you want to see a fool in the country, bring one with you!!

A stout heart and a muck fork

The farming year started in March, weather permitting, with muck carting. Manure was loaded into the cart and taken into the meadows starting four or five yards from the walls in the corner nearest the gate. We opened the door at the back of the cart, lifted it off its hinges and left it there to be picked up after unloading. At this point a heap of manure was pulled out of the cart with a muck rake. We then moved on in line with the wall another five yards and pulled out another heap and so on. Usually the cart carried eight heaps and the rear door was picked up as you went back for another load.

When the meadow was covered with the neatly set out heaps in rows five yards apart, it was muck spreading time. To do this you needed a stout heart and a muck fork. Going to the first heap, you flung the manure with a flick of the wrist and then thoroughly scattered the muck evenly over the grass, carrying on till the field was done - or you were.

My Dad used to spread muck for other farmers. The pay was sixpence a score. Just think of it - two and a half new pence for spreading twenty heaps of manure, which was getting on for three tons.

After muck spreading came chain harrowing, a light job for a single horse. This broke down and levelled the manure still further, also levelling any molehills at the same time.

Sometimes stones would be carted out in the muck and you had to pick these off the meadow, for if they got into the mowing machine later, they could

cause great damage. I used to go up and down the fields with a bucket, collecting and tipping them into the gateway. While I did this Dad would be building up any gaps in the drystone wall.

Next came the rolling. The roller itself was made of stone with a wood and iron frame to which the shaft was attached for one horse to pull. On one occasion, Dad was rolling the big meadow, which had a footpath running through it, when seven or eight young teenagers came along, accompanied by Ron Lindley. Dad stopped Stella as the group drew near, to give her a rest and to have a word or two with Ron. The roller had become coated with a thick layer of soil and manure, just like a rolling pin when the pastry is too wet.

"Where have you lot been?" Dad asked. *"Down Churn Hole cutting hazel sticks to sell as walking and cow sticks,"* Ron replied. Dad took one off him, looked at it and then started to use it to push the clods off the roller. One or two of the teenagers joined in, then started pulling them off by hand and throwing them at each other. It broke out into a real battle. Ron, thinking it was time to go, collected his band together quickly and took them off towards Chelmorton.

Sam Proctor, Hoppin Farm, Hollinsclough.

A sheltered hollow

The Burrs lay in a sheltered hollow, catching all the sun. That must be why our crops were ready before the gardens up in Chelmorton. We sold a lot of market garden greens in spring and summer. There was no waste at all, for anything we could not eat was boiled up for the pigs.

We had a small garden at the end of the house in the well yard. It was a suntrap and things grew very well there if you gave it plenty of water. We had another garden at the top right hand side of the garden field and this garden was about forty feet square. Blackcurrant bushes grew on two sides, with a good patch of rhubarb in one corner and a sycamore tree in the other. This garden was a very old one, but would grow well.

In the third year we were at the Burrs, Dad kept turning all the pigs into the stack yard for them to dig it up with their snouts. Pigs love to root. After about three months of dense pig grazing and rooting, the croft looked like a battlefield. There was not a bit of green to be seen anywhere. The pigs were kept out in early Spring and as soon as

the site dried out, Dad had got hold of an old wooden beam horse plough and managed to plough the land, so it would dry out faster and be ready for making into a good seed bed to be rigged up ready for potatoes and cabbage

Luckily it was a dry early spring in late March and April, very dry. Dad made full use of this, working the ground with spring tine harrows that we managed to get from somewhere. When he had got the soil broken down to his liking, we hooked Stella onto the ridge plough and I had to lead Stella up and down the croft in straight lines parallel with the wall. We made ridges on three quarters of the croft, the whole being about the size of a football pitch as I said. It took all Saturday afternoon - I remember I was very tired going round my hens that night.

We were up early at about 5.00 am the next morning - with it being Sunday, Dad was home for the day. As I came back from letting out and feeding my hens,

I caught Stella and brought her limping into the yard. She had no need to worry for she would have an easy day. All she had to do was pull the cart down from the muck heap to the croft and down the ridges that we had made ready, while we had to load the cart at the muck heap and unload it into the ridges. This was repeated time and time again until all the ridges had a good thick layer of manure all along the length of them. By dinnertime we had done twenty ridges.

While we were having dinner, Uncle Mo came, *"Where is George?"* I asked. *"Oh, he's following with his mother and Barbara somewhere."* Dad, seeing his chance to get some help, said to Uncle Mo, *"Can you use a ridge plough?" "Of course I can,"* he said. *"Good",* said Dad, *"Give him a drink. Do you want anything to eat?" "No, just a drink for now will do."*

After a drink of tea, Dad and Uncle Mo put plough pads on Stella, hooked her to the plough and split the rows back; so burying the manure. After the twenty ridges were done, Dad unhooked and unharnessed Stella and turned her out into the big meadow. Off she went, her lameness forgotten. A good afternoon's work had been done.

Ma and Aunt Winnie had got tea ready, so, after washing our hands, we all sat down to a fine meal, after which my Cowdale relatives set off home, to walk through Deep Dale, on through King Sterndale and then on to Cowdale.

Dad and I now got the wheelbarrow and loaded it with four boxes of seed potatoes. I got a bucket and digging spade and off we went into the croft and on to the headland to the end of the rows. We filled the bucket with potatoes. Dad got the spade and digging it into the top of the ridge, pushed the shaft forward leaving a gap in the soil into which I put a potato, and so on all down the ridge at about eighteen inch intervals. When the bucket was empty, I dashed off back to the barrow for more. We managed to plant the whole area with potatoes, to be followed by other vegetables and salad, as we got the chance, such as cabbage, cauliflower, sprouts, turnips, parsnips, celery, carrots, beetroot, peas, broad beans, runner beans, leeks and onions. Cucumbers and marrows were grown in frames made from old windows, and even tomatoes flourished in the well yard at the end of the house where they were out of the wind and caught the sun all day

By Whitsuntide, we had our first produce ready - broad beans, peas and early potatoes. To transport it to the village Dad made me a handcart. We did not make much money, for the great slump was on and there was very little money about. I suppose we were better off than most though, never being short of good fresh food.

After Harvest, with all the crops lifted, we took stock. We now had enough potatoes, swedes, carrots, onions, parsnips and other things to last all winter, making us far more independent and confident. A bit of land, hard work and foresight goes a long way to sustain a family.

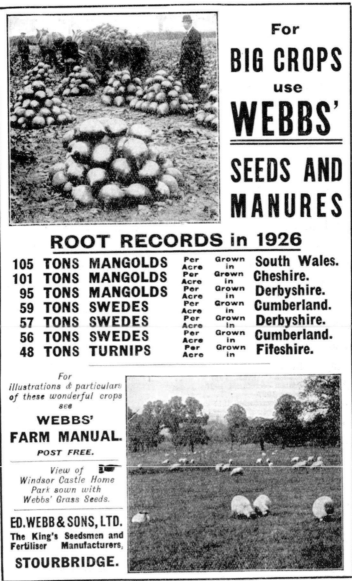

A lot of twiddling of knobs

One Sunday morning one of my Dad's friends called Herbert Ely came into the yard bringing a wireless in his car to sell to my Dad. After some bartering, they carried it into the house.

It took a long while to set it up. Earth wire, with an old copper water bottle fastened to the end of it, was buried in the ground outside the house window. The aerial was taken out of the window, up the side of the house, and across the yard, the end fastened to the top of the barn. It was about a hundred feet in all. Next we needed a dry battery and an accumulator, which had to be charged once a week and had to be carried to Chelmorton and left there for four days. It was a help to have two, as then you could take a flat one and return with a charged ready-to-go battery. After all was prepared and with a lot of twiddling of knobs, faint music came out. It was the first wireless I had ever heard.

An old wireless accumulator.

On winter nights, we always tried to get finished and into the house by 7.00 pm. If the batteries were still charged, we liked to listen to a programme called Inspector Thornley, as well as to Dick Barton and the News. I remember the batteries would always run flat at the most interesting part. At least when they did, we talked to one another again, instead of just listening to a box.

Summer was here

Hay-making time came round. Uncle Norman came to mow the meadows, one after another. He then turned the grass with a swathe turner. When it was dry, it was raked into rows with a raking machine and then we put the rows into heaps ready to cart. We had fitted the cart with raithes and gormers to hold a lot of loose hay. My Dad taught me how to load while he pitched it onto the cart, I got so good at loading that, when I was nine, I got work loading hay for other farmers at five shillings a week and as much excellent food as I could eat.

Hay-making was the biggest task on the hill farms before the 1939-1945 war. The grass was cut when the signs were right for good weather to come. There were no forecasts on television and radio could not be relied on. So we listened instead to what the older, wiser people had to say, and then we made our own minds up. This was done by watching the sky, the early morning dew and the animals, both wild and domestic. Plant life could also tell us a lot if we could read the signs. We watched and listened to our elders to gain their experiences; we watched and listened to the birds, the animals and the insects, for they knew when a change in the weather was coming.

While we were waiting for the right weather, the mowing machine was taken out of winter storage, cleaned and oiled, and the knives were sharpened ready. The sharpening of a knife made a lot of difference if done by a man who knew his job. If sharpened properly it cut clean, leaving a neat swathe and the mower was easier for the horses to pull.

Early one morning, often at about 4.30am, when everything was right and ready, the horses would be harnessed and hooked to the mowing machine. We took a spare sharp knife in a special wooden box, a hay fork and a rake, and set off for the first meadow to be mown.

Just through the meadow gate you turned the horses to the left until they were parallel with the wall, eight or nine feet away. You stopped your team, removed the fork, rake and spare knife to leave by the gate; you unfastened the cutter bar and let it down (upright when travelling between fields). You checked your horses, got on to the machine seat, got hold of the reins, put the machine in gear and as you moved forward, dropped the cutter bar the last foot onto the field. Away you went, keeping eight to nine feet from the wall all the way round.

Returning to the starting point, you kept straight on. Your left hand horse would now be walking on the mown grass and the other horse in the cleared gap between the standing grass and cut swathe, cleared by a grass board fastened on the end of the cutter bar. This pushed the cut grass to one side, leaving neat rows for the haymaking machines. You carried on until enough was cut or your horses need a rest. At this point, you lifted the cutter up just enough to miss the swathes, put the machine out of gear and returned to the gate where you started. If no one has gone to do it for you, you now tied the horses to the gate, got your rake and set off raking out the back swathe in the opposite direction to which you had mown it. If you were good enough you could do this as fast as you could walk. This done, you mowed the same way as you raked it, going twice round the field, all the grass up to the wall. Now it was best to change the knives because of hitting the odd stone on your way round this back swathe.

The break in mowing round the meadow used to give the young hares and other wild creatures chance to escape. Farmers were at one with nature, looking after it; they thought if you did not look after the wild life and plants, they would not look after us. How peaceful things were then. We did not know there was

a war coming to change all that. The sound of the horse-drawn mower was something that neither I, nor anyone else who was fortunate enough to hear it, would ever forget. The chatter of the knife could be heard from a long way off and yet even when you sat on the machine, you could hear the birds over this chatter. The sound told you that Summer was here. It made you feel excited and good. It put a feeling of urgency into you, for once the grass was cut, it had to be made into hay, dried and carted into the lofts, barns or stacks.

After the field was mown, it was left to wilt for one or two days, depending on the heat of the sun. When judged to be right, you put one horse into the shafts of a swathe turner. A swathe turner is a machine made to turn two swathes a time, as it is pulled round the meadow. The rear wheels were the drivers of the tines which turned the swathe. With a gear mechanism on each, the tines on each side could be turning in either direction. If both were turning clockwise round the field, the swathes would be turned away from the centre so if it had to be turned again you would then either drive anti-clockwise round the field, or change the gears on the wheels by using the gear levers, which were easily reached from the driving seat. So then the lines turned anti-clockwise and the swathes would be turned back towards the centre.

If the crop was not too heavy, two turnings were usually enough. On the fourth or fifth day after cutting, you put the right hand set of tines in gear to turn clockwise and the left to turn anti-clockwise, thus putting two swathes in one. These were called windrows and left to dry.

Now you would get the raking machine, another one horse job, and rake the windrows into larger rows of hay. People would use two tined long shafted forks (hay forks) to make these into heaps ready to be loaded onto carts fitted with raithes and gormers to hold more, or onto four-wheeled drays with gormers, and taken back to the farmyard to be moved into the lofts or into barns. When these were full, we had to make stacks outside.

To load hay is a skilled job. You usually take your horse and cart to the far end of the field, with one man on either side of the cart and start pitching the heaps of hay on to the cart using pitching forks (long strong hay forks) with a boy or girl on the cart to load it. The first two heaps of hay go on the front corners of the cart, then one goes in between them, with the middle pushed and pressed down by the loader. The same pattern continues all the way to the back of the cart, then starts again at the front and so on until you have a load, or have reached the gate out of the field.

Reaching the farmyard, one man gets on the load and two get in the barn or loft, the man on the cart picking it off in the opposite way to which it has been loaded. In other words, the one who starts at the back, works to the front, picking the rear centre off first, then the corners and so on. If loaded properly, it is easier to unload. The people in the loft take the hay away from the picking hole (where the men on the cart put it) and pass it back for the other to 'mew' (shake and level). When a lot of hay is put together it gets very hot with internal heat and it can, and does, set on fire if it contains too much moisture.

Making a haystack is much more skilled. It has to be built to turn the weather i.e. the rain, wind and snow. While building you keep the centre higher but still keep the general shape. As the stack gets bigger, you have to watch out for it slipping or leaning, using stack props to steady it until it has got hot and settled. When the stack is built, you get a load of green grass and place it along the top to help stop wind damage. Next, you pull all the loose hay off the sides and then thatch the roof. A well-built and thatched stack is a credit to the farm. When all this has been done - let it snow, let it snow, let it snow!

Once the hay was all safely inside or stacked, we used to have a harvest supper, and that was something to remember. On some farms you got supper every night and what a spread they put on, while other farmers' wives worked in the field alongside the men; some of them did as much work too. In this case, you still got a good supper, plainer but very good, usually a ploughman's lunch type. There was always drink laid on - jugs of tea, bottles of beer and soft drinks. If you worked all day, you either went to the farmhouse, or baskets of food were brought to the field in which you were working. The pay may not have been high but the food was the best. Needless to say, the farmers who did not feed you were left to get their own hay in.

When one farmer was finished, he would take men and carts to help a neighbour who had not, especially if it looked like rain. If, through no fault of your own, you got behind or in a jam, a helping hand would come from somewhere.

First wages

The shortest month for grass on the pastures is August, so my summer holidays were spent taking the cows and calves out into the local green lanes to graze. My job was to look after them, not letting them stray too far and keeping them off the main roads.

First I took them to the left out of the top gate, then right into the lanes where the gypsies camped. I then turned them to the right out of the gate and down Dead End Lane. I carried a strong knife to dig for pignuts and I picked blackberries, wild strawberries and raspberries out of the dale.

I worked my way past the far side buildings to where the lane divides into two dead end lanes. Just above this point was a small field with a wide flat plank instead of a gate, which stretched across the gap in the wall about two foot six inches from the ground. Knowing the cows would not be able to go astray without passing this point, I lay on the plank for a rest.

Mr Bagshaw owned the field beyond the plank which he had recently ploughed and where he was growing turnips. I liked raw turnips, freshly picked. Looking the field over I saw a lot of tall weeds growing, the small ones unable to grow with the turnip tops shutting out the sun. I did nothing the first day but on the second I started pulling out the long weeds till I had an armful when I took them to the side of the gateway and put them onto a heap.

After two and a half days' steady work, there were no weeds to be seen amongst the turnips at all. Near the top of the field I had seen three turnips growing together. There was a large one with two small ones on either side. Giving the larger one a twist, I pulled it out and left the other two to grow more easily. I took my prize to the top of the field, peeled it and then lay on the plank on my tummy to feast and keep an eye on the cows who, by now, were 'eaten up' and ready for a move to another lane.

I had about half eaten my prize when out of the blue came a swishing sound and a rather nasty sting across my backside. I must have jumped two feet in the air and I landed in the field, turning to see what on earth had happened. I saw Mr Bagshaw with a riding crop in his hand. *"I don't grow turnips for you to eat without asking"*, he snapped. Then, taking two paces towards me, he saw the heap of weeds I had collected, but, taking little notice of them, he said *"Now show me where you got my swede from"*. I had the place marked well in my mind so that when I had finished pulling weeds, I could find it easily. I took Mr Bagshaw straight to the spot and he looked at the place where my swede had come from and knew that, if it had been left there, he would only have harvested one, for the other two could not have survived, but now they would do so until the Autumn when he would have two instead of one. He never mentioned the crack he had given me, but he said I had made a good job of the weeding. With that he got on his horse Charlie and road off towards Chelmorton.

Next day I took the cows down towards Far Ditch on the bottom lane. About mid-day Mr Bagshaw arrived on Charlie. *"You've taken a lot of finding."* *"Yes,"* I said, rubbing my backside. He rooted in a big pocket on the inside of his jacket and pulled out a large brown paper bag which he handed to me. Then he spun Charlie round and was gone. I did not open my bag until I had found somewhere comfortable to sit and then I carefully looked at what he had brought me. It was a drawing book with pencils and crayons, a bar of Cadburys, a large bar, a very large bar, which I put in the shade to take and share out at home. Also in the bag was a white envelope on which was written WAGES. I opened it and to my amazement, there was a crisp ten shilling note. I danced up and down with glee and then I saw Mr Bagshaw watching from some distance - probably to make sure I had not missed the envelope.

Later in the 30's, two houses were built by Mr Arden about half a mile from the Burrs. At least we could now see that someone was up in the morning by the chimney smoke or in at night by the distant lights. One of these houses was taken by Mr and Mrs Devlin who came from Stalybridge and were in their late fifties. Mrs Devlin asked my mother if I would collect their paper when I went to the village and she agreed. I got threepence a week and some sweets for the job and she used to bake marvellous muffins, six of which she sent me home with every Friday night.

Another little part-time job I had when I was rather older was blowing the church organ at Wormhill. You lifted a wooden handle up and down, something rather like a blacksmith's hearth bellows. But this job didn't last long because, from where I sat down at the side of the organ, I could see the choirgirls in the pews opposite, with no one except them able to see me. I used to pull faces at them, making them laugh when they were supposed to be singing. After a while, the Vicar realised what was happening so I lost the job. It was only ten shillings a year (50p in today's money) and that was for going three times on Sunday and once during the week - and it interfered with my farm work. Getting washed and changed three times on a Sunday was too much for me!

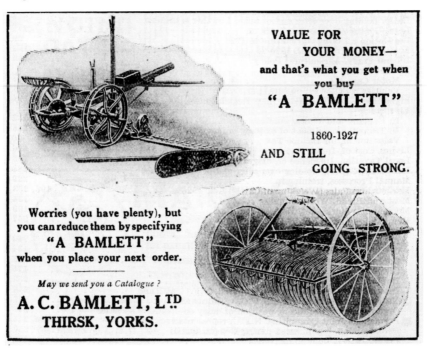

VALUE FOR
YOUR MONEY—
and that's what you get when
you buy
"A BAMLETT"

1860-1927
AND STILL
GOING STRONG.

Worries (you have plenty), but
you can reduce them by specifying
"A BAMLETT"
when you place your next order.

May we send you a Catalogue ?

A. C. BAMLETT, L.TD
THIRSK, YORKS.

Deepdale.

We trudged miles

Mr Barlow used to be the postman in those days. It was a nice job in good weather if you liked a ten-mile walk six days a week, up and down steep, rocky paths and over open fields from one farm to another.

With children using some of the same paths, farmers built stiles through or over the walls to help the postman and the schoolchildren and to save them going round by the lanes or through gateways which were, and still are, very muddy because of the cows going back and forwards. They could get so deep that a child could easily get stuck, so a network of private footpaths was created. Since then certain bodies, who knew no better, on seeing these paths with stiles have had them put on the O.S. maps as public rights of way. They are not and never were public footpaths.

Yet again, here and there, some unscrupulous farmers have closed public footpaths, bridle paths, packhorse tracks and green lanes. In the case of the latter, the walls have been removed, so as to add valuable land to their own, but in doing so, they have destroyed not only the ancient rights of way but also the rich plant and wild life that prospered in the lightly grassed and well sheltered lanes. All these injustices must be looked into and put right, for both the farmer and walker. And some of us country folk must continue to be vigilant, for the rights of future generations are at stake.

As I got older, my Dad took me round Churn Hole and showed me where Mr Hallam had his garden. It was about 30 yards square, between two cliff faces, with a fifty-foot sheer drop at one end, a perfect place for a secret garden. Only the narrow path gave it away but there were also so many fox and other animal tracks around it leading to nowhere in reach of man that it would confuse all but the wisest country person. .

At the base of the cliff, below the garden, was a wide but hidden cave about six feet high and twenty feet long. It was dry and warm, a perfect place for a highwayman to stable his horses. It is said that Robin Hood used it as a hiding place and for stores!

We moved round into Deepdale and Dad showed me the grazing paddock where packhorses had their overnight resting places. We went onto Dawson Cave which was probably an old lead working, below Swanclose Fields. Further on we crossed the Chelmorton to King Sterndale footpath and at the side of that was another cave which had also been used for lead-mining. On the opposite side of the dale I could see a larger cave mouth called Nettle Cave and then round the corner and opposite, right in front of me, was a cave which really took my breath away and which was the biggest cave I could imagine.

We sat in the entrance for a while. It was so peaceful there, until suddenly a strange noise came from down, down in the earth. My Dad had heard it when

Big Cave, Deepdale.

we first sat down but he waited until I heard it myself to see what I made of it. If I had been on my own I would have been half way home by now! The noise grew louder and then I realised there were voices coming from way down in the cave. Eventually a group of young people appeared, their clothes caked with clay, carrying torches and blinking as they reached the sunlight.

My Dad greeted them with a very good telling off for not leaving someone at the entrance, or at the very least, a very obvious note to explain they were in there, in the case of sudden flooding or roof fall. No one would ever have known where to look for them. It is another lesson I have not forgotten - and I bet they haven't either.

We moved on up the Dale to the bridle path that goes from King Sterndale Church to Chelmorton Church, called the Parson's Way. This we followed back to one of the green lanes that leads onto Caxterway, and then homewards. I was very tired and hungry by now.

Sometime later I was to experience the kind of tiredness that few people will ever know. There was deep snow on the ground and Grandad had sent some prize sheep to the Burrs which had gone missing. My Dad and I set out to look for them. We trudged miles, so it seemed. We went as far the Crewes fields on top of Deepdale. There was still no sign of the sheep.

Then, a blizzard sprang up. There was no shelter at hand, the nearest was Mr Bagshaw's far side buildings, so we made our way there. When we got to

THE BURRS IN WINTER

the building, Dad opened a door on the sheltered side and we got in but it was very cold and night was fast approaching. We could see The Burrs about half a mile away but it might as well have been ten with the snow. .

After a short rest we decided the best thing to do was to make straight for home, but there were eight walls to get over, simple enough normally, but the wind had blown the snow up in drifts against them, up to five feet deep.

We managed to make very slow progress until we were crossing a big field, where the snow had blown off it, leaving only a few inches on top, and we went along quicker. But at the next wall we paid for it, for the snow was up to five feet deep for twenty yards on either side. By the time we got to the fourth wall, I was shattered. This was a lower wall, and the snow not so deep, and at the fifth wall too. The sixth wall had four feet of snow for fifteen yards either side but once over that, we were on our own ground.

At last we got to the seventh wall, the one into the yard. Dad got over it and started to make a track for me to follow to get over the wall. I somehow climbed onto the wall and lying across the top, I fell asleep, there on top of the wall. My Dad came back for me but could not waken me but he managed slowly to carry me into the house. It was the next morning before I came to. Think on when you next think you're tired!

An old engraving of Chelmorton church.

Good sweet water

While we were at the Burrs we had several strange visitors. First, we had two Americans who came to find their ancestors' original home before they left for America in the late 18th century.

Another visitor was a Mr White, a very old man who said he had lived in the Burrs when he was a boy. He had left in about 1870 when he was ten years old. It was midsummer when he visited us. Ma made him a drink and sandwich, and seeing that she had got the water from a milk churn, he asked, *"Do you have to cart water in?"*.

We told him that there was no supply to the farm except rain or dew but he explained that they were never short of water sixty years ago and said they had a barrel well in the hollow of the field in front of the house, which was always running over with good sweet water.

Dad was very interested in this piece of news when he got home from work. On Saturday afternoon he took a spade and bar about five foot long and off he went to the hollow in the garden field to find any trace of well or water. A lot of work yielded nothing except some nice fossils, so the search for water was given up.

Years later I realised that the old man had got confused and maybe the house had changed, for a kitchen had been built onto what is now the back of the house

CHURN HOLE

and the door from the house into the kitchen was probably the front door in the past. In other words, the hollow in front would have been the one half way up the big meadow. On a closer look, sure enough there were signs of water. The plentiful supply of water must have been in the hollow which crosses the meadow, the well being close to the wall on the right hand side. If Dad had looked there we would have had water all right.

The Burrs farmhouse is very old, the walls are five feet thick at ground level tapering to four feet six further up, then three feet higher up still. It would be reasonable to suggest, judging from the age of the church at Chelmorton, that The Burrs is the only house left standing from the old village that stood a quarter of a mile down the valley until 800 years ago but which then moved to where Chelmorton stands now. The reason for the move is said to have been the shortage of water at the original site, whereas a spring near the Church at the top of Chelmorton supplied all that was needed there.

But, assuming there is indeed a source of fresh water at the Burrs, why did they really move the village from one site to another? If you stand on the high ground the other side of the farm and take a good look at the lie of the land, you can follow this long hollow across four or five fields in the direction of the settlements. It must indeed have been dug to carry water to the old village, so why did they move from one site to another? Could it have been for reasons of plague or land quake? There is a big fault in the rock under the valley and there could have been subterranean movement. Or is it possible that the Burrs was once a Manor House, the lord controlling the water and charging a tax on it? Or perhaps he built a dam to use the water for his cattle and irrigation. Perhaps a historian or archaeologist will come up with something positive one day to tell us.

A likely place for early man

In the early thirties, a gentleman came down the footpath past the Burrs, heading down into Churn Hole, and returning again in the evening. The same thing happened the next morning.

My Grandad was staying with us for a few days and after dinner, he went to where a large gap of the wall had fallen down during the winter. Near to the footpath he began to rid out the gap, moving the heap of stones that had been part of the drystone wall before it fell and so creating a gap which gave him room to pull out the big foundation stones and re-set them. As he moved the stones back, he set them out. Furthest to the back, he put the coping stones in a neat row, then the smaller stones, so that the nearer to the wall base they got, the bigger they were. The wall was then ready to be rebuilt, beginning with the big stones in the lower part of the wall.

Grandad was very interested in fossils and the limestone there was particularly rich in them. There are some good ones to be found while building walls. Finding a particularly good one amidst the heap of stone, Grandad placed it on the coping stone, telling me not to touch it.

"What is it for?" I wanted to know. *"Wait and watch and you will learn something later"*, he replied.

Ma brought us a drink and a small cake each at about 3 o'clock. After finishing his drink and eating his cake, Grandad picked up the stone he had placed on the coper and pointed out to me the fossils in it. *"If my theory is right,"* he said, *"We shall learn a lot today, because of that stone"*. And he put it back.

At about five o'clock, the archaeologist came back up the footpath. When he was about fifteen yards away, Grandad greeted him and moved from where he had been working onto the footpath. They introduced themselves and shook hands. The archaeologist was very interested in the way a drystone wall was built, saying what a good job Grandad was making of it. Grandad replied that it was hard to fit the stones so that they showed a good face to the outside, as most of them were a bad shape for building with. *"Don't you use a builder's hammer?"* *"No, the stone will get small enough with weathering, without using a hammer,"* Grandad replied.

Sam Swindell
wall-building near
the Burrs.

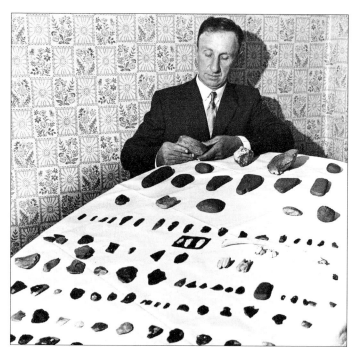

Artefacts found
around Deepdale.

Grandad turned to me, *"Fetch me that stone, will you, Claude"*, and I knew that he meant the one with the fossils in it. He handed it to the archaeologist, and I watched and listened. He was delighted with what he saw, telling us what the fossils were called and how old they were. He took off his rucksack, opened it and started to lift old stone-age flints out. He placed them on the ground, telling us all about them. Now Grandad had studied fossils and stone-age artefacts from books, but he was watching and listening and learning too. He asked where they had been dug up from but the archaeologist would not say.

"I can get you buckets full of things of that nature. Where are you staying?" asked Grandad. *"At the Church Inn,"* he replied. *"I think I will come up and see you later on and we can have a crack about where to find such things"*. With that, he collected his treasures, put them in his rucksack and off he went, up the footpath.

Ma called us in for tea and, a few minutes later, Dad came home from work. After tea, Grandad picked up a bucket and small spade, then down the path to the dale he went. An hour and a half later he was back, the bucket now part full of flints and stone tools of various descriptions. He got washed and changed, picked up the bucket and set off to the Church Inn to meet his man and hand over the contents of the bucket into what he thought would be safe hands.

For years after I tried to find out where he got those flints from. I know he went down to the dale for them but Grandad, in those days, was a very good walker and on reaching the top of the dale may have gone straight on down to Topley Pike Quarry. The likeliest place there would be on the baring tip. (As the quarry advanced the top and sub-soil were removed to leave bare rock. Topsoil was taken to one tip, sub soil and clay to another, to keep them separate. As the tipped soil was washed away with the rain, it would leave stones behind, to be seen and easily collected.

But if that was where they came from, they should have had clay and subsoil on them. So there again, perhaps he had turned left and gone on to the caves where fox and rabbit, digging and rain could have exposed his find.

Or he could have turned right and gone on to Mr Hallam's garden. For while Mr Hallam was digging and cultivating, he had a box into which he threw smaller stones as he dug them up. When the box had enough weight for him to carry, he would take it to empty onto a stone heap, thus keeping his garden tidy.

To him, a stone was a stone. He did not know that a flint stone might have been carried into his garden thousands of years ago by Stone Age man as a valuable tool. If Grandad had gone there and sorted through the stone heap, there was a good chance of finding what he had in his bucket. After all, in the past, it would have been a perfect place to live or find shelter, with protection on three sides by cliffs and the fourth protected even more easily, being a fifty-foot drop.

Yes, I think that would have been a likely place for early man to have chosen to stay, leaving behind him broken and blunt tools.

After that watching and listening lesson, I was always been on the lookout for such things but did not find anything of merit until September 1st 1943. We were ploughing on Wormhill Moor in the Autumn and after leaving the furrows exposed all winter to the frost, wind and rain, I went back the following spring to make a seed bed ready for oats to be sown.

I noticed three dark circles about twelve feet or more across of much darker soil. Stopping and getting off my tractor, I went to investigate and lying all around exposed and washed by the weather were flint scrapers, knives and other miscellaneous items. I picked up what I could, using a bag off the tractor seat and, after putting the bag and its contents back on the tractor, I carried on cultivating all day.

I later found more scrapers in a field below Wormhill but no trace of any settlements. I also have an iron-age quern for the handgrinding of corn and one Roman coin marked X Caesar Constantine.

The huntsman's horn

The hunt met at inns all over the Peak District, usually twice a year, at each place during the season from October to February. Although it offered a spectacle, they seldom caught a hare or fox.

A column would be placed in the local newspaper by the hunt committee giving a calendar of where and when hunt meetings would take place, mainly for innkeepers and farmers to know when to expect the invasion. Farmers would then move their stock into well-fenced home fields so that the horses and hounds would not scatter them.

On the morning of the hunt which was either a Wednesday or a Saturday, horse boxes, trailers and cattle trucks would start arriving from 9.00 am. They parked at the side of the road, leaving the parking space near to the inn where toilets and refreshments might be available for the cars that followed. Not that the hunt followers ever spent much - as one landlord once told them, they left more behind than they drank.

The groom unloaded and saddled the horses, and then led them to the inn where the gentry would be assembled in their best hunting suits. Ten minutes before the start, the hounds were unloaded from a cattle truck, to busy themselves fouling the whole area around where they were unloaded. When the appointed time came, the Master in charge blew his hunting horn. The hounds started baying and bang, off they went.

When they met at the Church Inn at Chelmorton, they would leave by going up Church Lane on one occasion and along Common Lane on another, then through a gate that would be opened for them by the hunt followers on foot. A lot of the villagers used to follow the hunt, the adults to laugh at the gentry being outwitted by the hare or the fox - cheering the wild animals when this happened.

The children were there for the money, for when you opened a gate for them, you got one or two pennies. You quickly closed it behind them in case another hunter came along, when you repeated the performance and got more pennies! On a good day you could make up to 10 shillings, as much as a married man with two children got on the dole for one week.

One Saturday morning, when I was eight or nine, I first heard and then saw the hounds and horses galloping across Mr Grindey's fields towards the Burrs

ground. I saw them jumping over the walls where they were low enough or where there was a gap but two riders came down the little lane towards the Burrs. The little lane had a gate where it ended and opened into our little meadow. Seeing my chance for spending money, I ran to the closed gate and opened it just before the huntsman and huntswoman reached it. They did not speak but threw two pennies down into the mud. As the lady rider went off across the meadow she turned around and laughed at me, rescuing the pennies out of the mud. I decided there and then that horses are far nicer than some of the people that ride them.

I watched them go through the gateway into the big meadow, across over the low wall into Goulds and across two fields. They were coming up to a high wall with no gaps. They turned left following the wall up the field until a low place was found and jumped over into Mr Bagshaw's land. By this time, all the other hunters had disappeared so these two individuals made their way across to the large plantation. I quickly made my way over in that direction, thinking they were heading for the gate at the far end of Mr Bagshaw's land and out onto the lane.

Perhaps I would have the chance of more money. As I was passing the plantation, I saw the two horses near the wall which went round it but where were the riders? Going quietly between the horses and looking over the wall, there they were, and they seemed to be wrestling.

The lady said *"But someone may see the horses."* At this point I chirped up, *"Don't worry, I'll look after them for you."* They didn't seem very pleased to see me peeping over the wall, nor did they give me anything for my trouble. Indeed, they were quickly gone.

I did not get much money out of it but I had seen a bit of life; and still had the satisfaction of knowing that she only laughed at me once, while their surprise at seeing me looking over the wall at them will be, and has been, laughed at for a long time!

When Dad got home from work I told him all about what had gone on during the day. He was annoyed about the two pence being dropped in the mud and one of them laughing at me having to pick it out. He said, *"Let them open and close the gate themselves in future"*. The majority of the hunt members treat what appear to be rough labourers with respect knowing full well that some of them are tenant farmers, while others own the land they farm and the hunt has to have their permission to ride over it.

With this in mind, Dad said no more about it until one day a gentleman came to the Burrs on a fine bay horse. He got down from his mount, shook hands with Dad, and wanted to know if the last season's hunt had done any damage. *"Well"* Dad said, *"In the main no, but the two riders that separated from the rest did,"* and he related all that I had told him. He was not very interested until Dad got to where I went between the rider-less horses at the plantation wall and saw the riders as I thought wrestling in the wood. Then he was very angry. *"Those two will never ride with this hunt again",* he said and he mounted his horse and galloped away.

It always comes to those that wait. It was not the twopence being thrown in the mud but the arrogant young lady up on her fine horse laughing at what she must have taken for the child of a labourer. Maybe I was but I was also the grandson of a landowner - the owner of the land she was riding on and only because permission had been sought and gained by better people than her.

As I said before, it is rare that anything is caught on a hunt, for the hare has many tricks to pull out of his hat, so to speak. When being chased by dogs, it will jump a high wall and in full flight it will turn somersault in mid-air to land facing the wall in the opposite direction, then turn left or right running along the wall. If it is uphill either way, it will take the uphill route, for a hare can easily out-run and lose hounds uphill. It is built for uphill work with its hind legs longer and stronger than its front. If the field into which it has jumped is flat, it will use well the thirty or more seconds it has won by changing direction under cover of the wall. When the hounds jump the wall after it, they go straight on and get two or three hundred yards before realising they have lost the scent and have to back-track to find it again.

Meanwhile John Hare is legging it for the dale. Once he makes the dale, the hounds have no chance of catching him, for on the steep sides of the dale with its cliffs, brambles and thickets of blackthorn and hazel, larger, heavier animals have no chance. He that runs away, lives to run another day.

It is only the old who are at risk. But the old are wise and usually move into the dales at the first sound of the huntmaster's horn, while the pack of hounds are still perhaps two miles away. Sound travels a long way in the country. It is the sickly ones that are caught, so helping to keep the hare population alert and healthy.

Once one hare has out-smarted the hounds, the others are fairly safe for by now the pack will be getting tired and if they get onto the scent after being fooled once, they don't seem to put their heart into the chase. The hares are lucky I suppose, having the shelter of the hills and dales so close, into which to escape.

There are many sides to the argument about hunting. The hunt used to bring some badly needed cash into the community, to the inn who took more staff for the day, for parking in farmyards, for stabling of spare mounts, for opening and closing gates, and most of all, for damaged walls and property. To those who do not know the whole story of hunting, the real pleasure for the onlooker is to be on high ground and to see for yourself a hare using its tricks to outwit the whole pack of twenty-five to thirty hounds, and twenty to thirty-five horseriders.

Perhaps you think the hare should be left in peace and hunting banned. Let me remind you Johnny Hare has to be kept on his toes, for if he is not, the fox and, worse still, the poacher will take over. They creep around in the very early morning while farmers are milking or feeding their cows, and all the year round where there are a lot of hares to be had. No my friends, keep the hunt, they only come in the season when the hares are not expecting or the young have grown, and they are warned of the approaching danger by the huntsman's horn. The poacher can, and will be about all the year round, and he is stealthy and clever.

.

White Peak Memories

Lady Maud Baillie and
the hunt at Church Inn.

Jack Gould and Tony
Chapman, School
Lane, Chelmorton in
the late 1930s.

The best trout she ever had

The first time I can remember going to Grandad's new farm we got up very early one Sunday morning. Ma lit the fire to boil the kettle, and while this was going on, I dashed off to feed and let out the hens from the safety of their hen cotes where they were shut up each night.

As I returned from this task, I could smell bacon frying on the open fire making me feel very hungry. By the time I got back to the farmyard, Dad had fed all the other animals and we went in for breakfast at about seven. After breakfast we got out his bike on which he had fitted a seat for me to ride with him, and we walked up the lane onto Coalpit Lane which was tarmac by now.

Dad put me into my seat, got on himself and away down the road we went at what seemed a very fast speed, with the wind blowing in my face and the walls and trees flying by. It was very exciting but when we started to go uphill, we had to get off and walk to the top before climbing on again. We got off three times because of hills. We went down Coalpit Lane to the Far Ditch, turned right onto Brierlow Garage Turn, then right onto the Ashbourne-Buxton Old Roman Road into Buxton. We went up Fairfield, on to Dove Holes, down to Chapel en le Frith, past the Cross Keys at Chapel Milton, landing in the Breck Yard at about 8.30am. From there we walked the last mile to Shireoaks along a rough lane with twelve gates to open and close, getting to Grandad's about 9.00am, just in time for another breakfast - and a good one too, home cured bacon, oatcakes, egg and fried potatoes.

When I had ridded my plateful, Grandad got up from the table and said, *"Come with me, me mon"*. When we got out into the yard Uncle Norman was loading the churns of milk into the two-wheeled milk float. Grandad and I climbed onto the float and he took up the reins, said *"Go*

on", and the horse was off at a trot down the lane to the first closed gate. I soon knew why he had taken me along with him; I could open and close the gates. *"Hop out and open that gate,"* he said. *"See as you close it properly after the float has gone through"*. I was quick to obey of course and the procedure was repeated at all the gates down and all the gates back. By the time Dad and I reached home that night, I had opened and closed gates 48 times, 50 counting the gates into the Burrs!

We had to get home before dark to get the hens shut up, before the foxes did their nightly rounds to see what was going cheap and easy. Dad had his animals to feed. I also had fire lighting sticks to take into the house and put on the shelf over the oven to dry out ready for next morning. When I told Ma how I had enjoyed the day out, she asked if I would like to go and stay at Grandad's for a while because she had to go into hospital for a few days. *"I would like it OK,"* I said, *"but I can't leave Dad on his own to do my jobs as well as his."* *"Oh, he will manage all right,"* Ma said, *" Besides, he will have to go to work and you can't stay here on your own all day"*. With that I decided to go to Shireoaks and stay with Grandad and Grandma.

All that week I was very busy cleaning out the hen coops, putting new hay in the nest boxes, getting lots of bundles of fire wood for lighting in a morning and anything else I could think of that would help my Dad while I was away. On Saturday morning, Dad got time off work because the quarries were slack as there were no orders for lime.

We got up early, fed the animals and had an early breakfast, but Dad told me not to let the hens out. We put some boards, short nails and chains into my handcart and off we went to the hen coops, Dad carrying the tools and the hen corn. When we got to the first hen coop Dad selected six boards of similar length, and made a tunnel with them and hung short chains from the roof of the tunnel. When all was in place, I opened the small door for the hens to come out, but now to get out they had to come through the new tunnel. Hens being hens, they would not come out through the new arrangement with chains to push past. To get over this, I got a handful of corn and scattered it along the tunnel floor and they were soon out following the trail.

"How will we get them in again?" I asked. *"That's no problem,"* he said. *"Now they have found a way out and know that the chains are safe, they will go*

in and out as before. But when a fox comes along and sees this arrangement, he will think trap and go on his way leaving the hens for another day."

"Does this mean we do not need to shut them up at night now then?" I asked. *"Well, if I am late home from visiting your Ma in hospital or forget them, they should be safe. The trouble is Foxy may wait outside the hen coop for the hens to come out early in the morning but if it does, it will grab the first one out and be gone. We will only lose one but if he could get into the hen coop, he would kill the lot. The fox knows that it always comes to those who wait. But if you find that one is missing and see feathers scattered around, you will know what has happened. Foxy will be bound to try the same thing the next morning, and while he is sat there watching and listening for a hen for breakfast, you can get within fifty yards with a shot gun and give him an early morning call of two ounce of lead. It always comes to them that wait!"*

Sure enough, when I went round at 6.00am to feed them and to collect the eggs they had been in and out to lay and when I went round again later to shut them up, they were all in, as happy as could be.

The next job was to get the small buckets and go into the well yard for water. Now in the well yard there was no well as you might suppose but a large pond, or mere as we called them, the rain water from the house roof being run into it. In dry weather, it was only fed by dew which was condensed on the flat paving stones of its floor and sides, collecting three to five gallons a night. The only time I saw it empty was when we cleaned it out in very dry weather and then only for a few hours for next morning it would have 6 inches of water back in from the dew. This supply was for household use and drinking until the mid 1930's, at which point we started carrying drinking water from Chelmorton.

My buckets filled with water, I took them to a homemade boiler at the bottom of the yard. After two or three trips the boiler was half full, and using a sheet of newspaper and some dry sticks, I lit a fire under it, slowly stocking it with larger and larger pieces of wood. Leaving it to get the water hot I went into the stack yard, now a very large garden, to collect cabbage leaves and shoots that grew on the cut cabbage stalks. These I put in the boiler together with a bucket of small and damaged potatoes, followed by a handful of salt taken from a 28lb block that was stored in a dry place in the hayloft.

I kept looking after the fire, getting the lot boiling, and keeping it so until it was cooked. When nearly cooked I normally stopped feeding the fire, leaving it to go out. When this lot was cool it was ready to feed to the pigs. Today I repeated the process several times, and Dad ladled the hot food out of the boiler into an old bath, enough to last all week.

While this was all going on, Ma had packed me a case containing spare clothes and other bits and pieces for my stay with Grandad, between getting dinner ready. On Sunday morning, getting near to the time to go, my conscience got the better of me again. I was thinking about Dad being left to do all the work on the farm, so I changed my mind and I did not want to go. (30 years later I would see the same thing happen with my children). Anyhow Mr Ely arrived in his car, a Morris 8, so, like it or not, I had to go. Saying my good-byes to Ma, I climbed unhappily into the car.

I was made very welcome at Grandad's. Uncle Norman partly took the place of my Dad by keeping an eye on me, and having him to turn to helped a lot. It was a fortnight before Dad came to see me on his solo motorbike. He brought Uncle Mo with him - if he had not, I would have demanded to go back with him and he knew it.

While I was at Shireoaks, Herbert taught me how to catch trout by hand. When I told Dad about this, he said jokingly, *"You can't catch fresh fish with your hands."* With this, off I went down to the brook. After about an hour, I was back with a good-sized trout. He was delighted and wrapped it up to take home with him. Ma was back at home by now so when he got back he gave her the trout telling how I had caught it. She cooked it in butter and said then, and always, that it was the best trout she ever had.

The next weekend Dad came to take me back to the Burrs with him. Grandma packed my case and gave me a parcel of baking, including some of her currant flat cake. I have never found any like or as good as hers in my life. The younger generation have tried but failed to make the same finished product.

Dad had improved the pillion seat on the A.J.S. motorbike putting a back rest and arms on it for more safety for a younger person to ride. Putting me in my seat and strapping my case on the back of it, we were ready to leave Shireoaks. To save Dad having to stop at each gate, Uncle Norman went on his bike to open and close them for us. It only took just over half an hour to get to the Burrs, going in across Caxterway Lane and through the gate into the top stable field. I climbed off to open the gate, and Dad went through and left me to close the gate and run down the two fields after him.

When I got to the house, I was in for a surprise. I had a new sister! I had very mixed feelings about it. But I had no time for baby sisters - I was off to check on my stock, to feed my hens and count them, and to collect some wood for lighting the morning fires on the way.

A baby at the Burrs.

A jar of flowers and a loaf of bread

As there were only a few days left before the Summer holidays I did not go back to school again that term. On Monday morning, I let out my hens and fed them, and then went back and had my own breakfast. Then I got my little barrow, brush and shovel, and went round all the hen coops to clean them out, wheeling the muck well away from the buildings and spreading it on the field.

As I was making my way back to the farmyard, I saw a lady coming down the little lane with three dogs on leads. She came across to the house, tying up the dogs before going in to see Ma and my sister. After about half an hour she came out, untied her dogs and off she went, the way she had come across the little meadow and up the lane. Curiosity overcame me so I went in to ask who she was. *"That is Nurse Webster,"* Ma said, *"She came to see if Baby and I were going on all right. She will be back next week."*

During the next few weeks I would get to know the nurse very well. She was a nice person, very knowledgeable of what was going on in the countryside, and she spent the little time she could spare talking to me about the farm. I suspected she would have liked to live on a farm.

I thought Ma would like some flowers, so away I went to an old green lane where I knew all kinds of wild flowers grew. I made a mental note of the flowers as I passed to pick them as I came back. Getting to the end of the lane and not seeing anything special, I went over into the dale to look at what was in bloom there. The cowslips had gone to seed but the orchids were in full bloom. The purple orchids with black spots were common but in a certain sheltered place, facing the sun, grew some very different ones. There were not a lot of them so I picked only three of the largest, then turned for home, making up my bunch with other flowers that took my fancy. As I went along the lanes on my way home I found a two-pound jam jar for a vase. I put some water in and set out the flowers. Ma was very pleased with them and put them on the window bottom.

The next day Nurse Webster came on her usual visit, and when she saw the three orchids among the jar of flowers she was very excited, saying how rare they were, normally only growing on the chalk along the South Coast, and asked me where I had got them. *"Oh"*, I said, *"About half an hour's walk away,"* not wanting anyone else to know where they grew. She did not ask any more, but looked at me for a few seconds. She said, *"You are very wise, Claude; the fewer people who know where they grow, the safer they are."*

As Nurse left, she told me she was doing a study of what different children did while on holiday from school. *"Would you write me a list of what you have been doing this next week for when I come again?"* I just looked at her and said nothing. When she came again, she asked me for my list. I said I had not made one but I could tell her if she wanted to write it herself. *"Oh no"*, she said, *"I want you to write it for me please."* At this point I had to admit I could not write. I thought she would have turned nasty or sarcastic like my teachers, but she did not. She just smiled nicely and said, *"We will have to see what we can do about that then won't we?"* and no more was said about it.

The next time she came she had a brown paper bag with her. After she had seen to Ma and Baby she turned her attention to me. She got me to sit at the table with her and opened a one-penny bar of Cadbury's chocolate which she placed in the middle of the table, saying nothing. Then she pulled out a pen and pencil. At this, I would have normally lost all interest and bolted for the door, but that bar of chocolate was too tempting. Then a book came out, to read and write in.

"What can you make of this?" she asked, handing me the book at the first page. It was a picture of an apple with apple written in large letters under it and a large A above. Taking up the pencil she pointed to the big A - *"what does that say?"* *"A for apple"*, I said. We went through the pages until we got to Z for Zebra. *"Very good. Now let's see what you can do without any pictures"*.

Turning the page, there was a simple little story and I read it to her with no trouble. After several short stories, we came to plain pages with only lines on them. She gave me the pencil and said, *"Now you write apple for me"*. I could do the big A and the small a, but that was all. *"You can do more than that, can't you?* she asked. *"No, I can't."* *"Of course you can"*. So I wrote APL. *"That is not quite right, is it?"* she said. But my mind was blank. Then I had a good idea. I could write chocolate and I did so, copying off the bar in front of me. *"Well,"* she said, *"You can certainly read and copy. Try the apple again. If you try harder, you get the bar of chocolate."* It was no use. All I could come up with was APL. She gave up, giving me the chocolate.

I did not learn to write until over forty years later. I had had an operation on my right knee and while I was housebound I was watching *On the Road* on

TV, a programme about someone who could not write, who decided to go to school for adult education. I thought this was a good idea, so I rang a neighbour, Mrs Kelly, who was a teacher, to see if she knew of a night school nearby that taught writing. She said she did not believe me when I said that I could not write. I told her it was true.

"*Oh,*" she said, and apologised. "*I did not mean it like that. I am actually teaching at the night school in Hyde tonight and have no transport, so if you want to go, you could give me a lift.*" I had adapted my car so that I could drive it with a bad leg, so, at the appointed time, I picked up Mrs Kelly, and to the night school we went. After enrolling, I went into the classroom where many students sat, all above thirty years of age. There were people in there learning to read and write, some of whom I knew, including business people who I never dreamt could not write. This gave me more confidence.

I was taken to a small room away from the others for assessment. I was asked if I knew the alphabet. I did. Could I read? I could. "*I just can't write,*" I said. So I was given paper and pen and asked to write about one of the pictures on the wall. They told me not to worry at all about the spellings at this stage.

On the wall in front of me were four pictures. The instructor asked me to write what I could about one of them and left me to it. I looked at the pictures for a few minutes. One was a car, one was a loaf of bread, next was a bottle of beer and the last one was a house. I chose the loaf of bread for my story, being very interested in history. I started off with the cultivation of wheat back in Ancient Egypt, bringing the story of wheat forward to 1945, using up two pages of foolscap to do so. I finished off with wheat ground into flour with the addition of salt, yeast, water, and heat to make bread.

Before I walked into that class room and saw others like myself, from all social classes, all learning to read and write, I dared not let anyone see my writing, for I thought I was the only one who could not spell. Now I did not care who read my writing. In this new frame of mind, I began to enjoy writing. Now I think - if it's spelt wrong, it takes a real scholar to read it!

After I had been back home about half an hour, the phone rang and a voice asked for Mrs Fearns. The night school manager was checking with my wife that I really could not write before my attendance at classes!

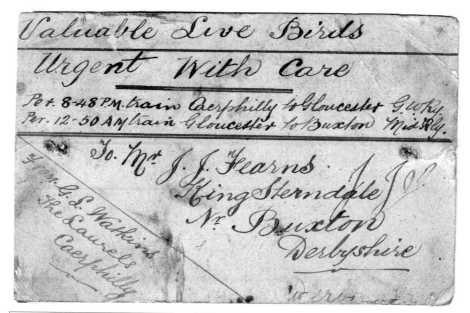

Rail and road transport.

We'll be all right for the winter now

During the school summer holidays of 1937, Dad thought it would be a good chance to go and visit Uncle Jim and Auntie Flo near Burton on Trent.

We now had a BSA 500cc motorcycle with a long sidecar. On the Friday night, dad serviced the motorcycle. He changed the oil, checked the tyres, plugs and points and made sure the tool kit was complete and the pump for blowing up the inner-tubes was in good working order, the lights working and the spare bulbs packed safely.

On Saturday morning, I fed and let out all the hens as always and by then breakfast was ready. After breakfast, I went to Chelmorton for anything that was needed and to collect Mrs Devlin's papers, delivering them to her on my way home. Mrs Devlin gave me threepence, some sweets and some homemade muffins.

When Dad got home from work at midday, we had dinner, then I rushed off round the hens again, giving them extra food while Dad gave the pigs extra rations. Ma had packed sandwiches and cakes to eat on the way and after a quick wash and change, she got into the sidecar with Joyce on her knee and Muriel in the small front seat. I opened the farmyard gate for Dad to drive through, closed it after him and climbed onto the pillion seat. Up the two stable fields to the top gate, open and close, climb back on pillion seat, and we were off. It was the first time we had all been out together. A great adventure.

We went along the top lane down Coalpit Lane to Far Ditch through Horse Dale, past Shallow Grange to Brierlow Bar Garage where we filled up with petrol. Young Sam Bagshaw was looking after customers' needs at the pumps and in the small shop. He was a real character in those days, very good natured and good humoured, the best of salesmen. Seeing Ma in the sidecar, who he had not seen for two or three years, he ignored Dad's request for petrol and went and had a few words with her, cracking a joke or two. There was a 'method in his madness', for he was also giving Dad time to look around at what else he had to sell - knowing full well that Dad could not go anywhere else for fuel as the next garage was miles away.

After a couple of minutes, he turned his attention to Dad, who was weighing up the R.O.P (Russian Oil Products) pump, where petrol was only tenpence a gallon. *"Will you try that today?"* asked Sam. *"No,"* Dad said, *"I'll have Cleveland"*. *"But that is one shilling a gallon,"* Sam protested. He must have been on a bonus to sell the R.O.P but Dad would have none of it. *"Cleveland is what I always have and Cleveland is what I want"*. With that Sam filled up the motorcycle and we were off south along the old Roman road, nowadays called London Road, towards Sterndale Moor, past the Quarries and on towards Ashbourne. We carried on through Ashbourne, still on the London Road towards Lichfield, going through Sudbury and on to the seven lane ends. Leaving the London Road behind us, we took the second left road at this junction towards Needwood.

A mile or so along this road, we stopped in a lay-by to have a rest and stretch our legs. Ma got the food and drink out and, while I was eating, I looked up and on the branches of the tree overhead were apples, and on another one, pears, and there were some trees with dark purple plums. I had never seen fruit growing before. It was fascinating so I asked Dad why we didn't grow fruit like those and he told me that we lived too high up for them to grow and ripen.

Suitably refreshed, in both belly and mind, we set off again, heading for Shobnall. At the crossroads, at Shobnall, we turned right up a minor road leading to the farm track, crossed a golf course and went up into the farmyard.

Uncle Jim had heard us coming up the hill and met us at the gate, looking very pleased to see us. As we pulled up at the garden gate leading to the house, Auntie Flo came out, followed by my cousins Dorothy and Barbara. Dorothy was the eldest, about two years younger than me, with Barbara one year younger still. We off-loaded and went into the house through the front garden, which was a blaze of colour.

As soon as I had hung my coat up, I wanted to get outside and explore. Uncle Jim took Dad and me out into his kitchen garden - a very large garden indeed. In fact, he used to plough it with horses instead of digging it by hand. With being further south and about 800 foot lower, the seasons were longer and warmer, so he could grow most things out in the open that we couldn't grow at all up in the high Peak District. There were tomatoes, cucumbers, marrows, onions as big as my Dad's fist, and strawberries. Beyond the garden was an orchard with pears, plums, apples and damsons.

They looked very inviting but they were guarded by thousands of wasps! Uncle Jim suggested my Dad picked some of the pears that were ripe to take home. *"Not bloody likely, not with all those wasps around." "'Ere, they wonna sting you,"* said Uncle Jim. *"No, but they have bloody hot feet!"* my Dad said. *"Never mind"* said Uncle Jim, *"Ike Billings is coming later to gather some for his wife to bottle, he might pick you some at the same time."*

Sure enough, in about half an hour, a very leathery gentleman arrived on his bike, had a word or two with Jim and Dad, then picked up a ladder and reared it into one of the pear trees. Next he pulled up his union shirt 'till it was baggy and blowing, undid his buttons and tightened his belt, and was ready for the pears. Off up the ladder he went, surrounded by a cloud of wasps. On reaching the fruit, he started plucking the pears and placing them inside his shirt, taking no notice of wasps at all. When he came down with a load of pears, we all stood well back for there were wasps all over him, crawling out of his shirt, up his neck and down his arms, but he ignored them completely, emptied out his shirt into baskets, moved the ladder and was off up for more.

After climbing down with the second lot, he moved the ladder again and invited Dad to go up and pick some for himself. *"Not likely,"* said Dad. *"There's nought to worry about unless you are afraid of heights,"* said Ike, *"Look, the wasps haven't stung me once."* Dad would have none of it. *"The pears'll have to stay there before I'll go up that ladder amongst that lot."*

Ike said if he was capable of totally ignoring them and getting on with the job of picking pears, they would certainly not sting him but if he once thought about it, they would attack. With that, up the ladder he went and collected us thirty or forty pounds of nice ripe pears to take home - although a lot got eaten, then and there.

At five o'clock Uncle Jim had to organise the milking of eighty cows by hand, a formidable task. Dad milked ten of them to help him get them done earlier. A good hand-milker can average one cow in four minutes by working hard and avoiding getting kicked. But if you do not know how to stop them doing it, they can send your bucket and stool flying.

After the work was done, we all sat in the garden drinking homemade wine. To keep the wasps away from the glass, they put a plate of wine on one side for the wasps to help themselves and cool their feet! The four little girls went to bed at seven o'clock, and I was sent up at eight, and with the drop of wine and a long day, I was soon fast asleep.

I woke up with a start around five to hear the dawn chorus. I had never heard so many birds before. Then somewhere closeby, I heard a fox call, reminding me that my hens had not been shut in last night. I hoped that the tunnel and chains Dad had made would frighten the fox. I had run my hands over the short chains hanging on the tunnel entrance to leave my scent so that Foxy would be very suspicious.

I turned my attention to my new surroundings and sound. I heard the noise of a spoon dropping into a cup or mug. Someone was up. Time for me to get up - I might get a brew. There was a lot to do. I must have a proper look around this place.

When I got downstairs, Uncle Jim was sitting with a pint mug of tea in front of the newly lit fire. *"Morning,"* he said. *"Did'st sleep well? Come and have a drink, there's plenty in th' pot. Gerra pot off theer and meck thee sen a brew, then tha can guw wi' may, fer th' milk cows"*. I made and drank my brew quickly and off we went for the cows.

The field in which they had spent the night was huge, the biggest field I had been in. By the time we had got the cows in for milking, other farm workers had turned up for work. They started at six o'clock. Although it was Sunday, it made no difference; the cows had to be milked, the milk collected as it was sieved and cooled, and put into 17 gallon churns, ready to be taken into the town for sale.

Among the 6.00 am starters was a youth about fifteen years of age who had nothing to do with the cows. He went and caught a strong pony which he harnessed and put into the shafts of a light grass cutter and went off towards the golf course. While I had been going round the field to drive the cows in for milking, I had spotted some mushrooms. With this in mind, I went to the house to find something to carry them in.

By this time Ma was up so I told her what I wanted. With Flo there to look after Muriel and Joyce if they woke up, Ma said she would go mushrooming with me, so with a basket each, off we went. It was a lovely morning for a walk anyway. We worked our way across the field where the cows had been, picking mushrooms as we went. Reaching the hedge on the far side and looking over in the next field, we saw a lot of large mushrooms. We were unable to get through here, so we walked along the hedgeside to find a gap. As we walked along, we came to a wild damson tree, loaded with fruit. We ate a few and carried on, looking for a gap, passing hazels covered in hazel-nuts and big blackberry canes laden with fruit, and still more damson trees.

After a quarter of a mile, we found a gateway into the next field, and closing the gate after us, we went through. Our baskets were soon full, so we turned for the house and a well earned breakfast.

As we walked across the last field before the yard, we could see all the front and one side of the house and it was huge. I said to Ma, *"What a big house Uncle Jim has."* She laughed, *"They only have a small corner. It all used to be a monastery where monks lived hundreds of years ago. Now there are two or three parts of it made into farmworkers' cottages and the rest is unused."*

I was ready for breakfast now - fried potatoes, mushrooms, fried bread, eggs and bacon. Afterwards, Uncle Jim took Dad and me to see his horses, six huge shires which were used to do all the draught work on the farm. Uncle Jim was the waggoner then, in charge of all the horses and the horse work. He did it until Uncle Jack went to work there some years later and then Uncle Jim took over the cows.

After the horses, Uncle Jim took us on a long walk around the farm, taking a clean bucket with him. When he got to an exceptionally good damson tree, he reached up and pulled down a branch to pick the damsons into the bucket, and we picked off one branch after another until it was full. And while we were

out, Auntie and Ma had been out and picked two large baskets of blackberries for us to take home.

After we had finished a very good dinner, we loaded the pears, plums, damsons and blackberries into the sidecar, and then tried to find room for Mum, Joyce and Muriel. It was alright for me sat on the pillion. By three we were loaded up and off, and by six we were home. I quickly nipped round feeding the hens and collecting the eggs - with not being collected the night before, the nests were full of them. By the time I got back, Dad had fed the pigs, and as he cleared them out, I gave them fresh straw for bedding. When pigs have been cleaned out and given fresh straw, they chase around with delight. Then we checked the cows, and finally went home for tea.

After tea and getting Muriel and Joyce to bed, Ma started again - peeling, and getting the gear ready for the fruit to be bottled. She finished the lot before going to bed and over the next two days she made jam, first of all the blackberries, then the plums, and the damsons last. I had to carry the sugar to make it all from Chelmorton on the Monday morning!

When I looked in the pantry, seeing all those jars of lovely jam lined up, I thought *"We will be all right for the winter now."* The trip to Sinai had been well worthwhile.

Uncle Jim's team binding.

Quite a hoot

A farmer we knew set off for the Church Inn one very dark, winter's night. As he crossed Coalpit Lane and climbed over the stile to take the footpath along the foot of Chelmorton Low, he thought he heard something behind him. Turning round, he could see nothing, so he carried on towards the Church Inn. After going another hundred yards, he heard it again.... a jingling noise. He stopped and turned round but again he could see nothing nor hear anything. The hair on the back of his neck was beginning to stand on end. All he could see were the lights of Buxton in the distance. He set off yet again, his mouth beginning to get very dry. He had not gone many strides when he heard it again. This time he thought that, if, when turning round, he bent down low, he would see who or what it was silhouetted against the Buxton lights.

So the next time the jingling came, he turned round quickly and bent down low to see what was following in his wake; but he could still make out nothing. But the jingling suddenly started again, louder and coming straight for him. Quick as a flash, he whipped round and made for Chelmorton as fast as his legs would carry him - I am sure that was when the first four-minute mile was achieved, across the foot of Chelmorton Low! He leaped over the wall into the road above the Church Inn, as if his trousers were on fire. He burst in through the door of the Church Inn, bolting it after him. His face was white as snow and he was several minutes before he could speak.

Finally, to the alarmed locals in the ancient inn, he told of the ghost that was after him. Two of the braver men in the pub got a stick each, unbolted the door and carefully went outside to investigate. They were only gone a couple of minutes but it seemed like hours to the assembled drinkers. When they came back inside, one of them said, *"What kind of dog have you got, Jud?" "A black and white cow dog,"* the terrified man said, *"....and we have a black one that is kept chained up in the yard." "Well your black dog has come for a pint wi'thee!"* And in came his black dog, dragging four feet of broken chain behind.

It had followed him and each time he stopped, the dog had stopped. When he stopped and bent down, the dog must have taken it as an invitation to run to him. At which point the master ran faster than the dog!!

A young man, whose great-grandson now lives not far from where I am living now, set off from Chelmorton early one winter evening. He was on an accustomed social round to one or two local villages within walking distance, that is within five miles or so of his home - nothing unusual in those days.

Now this young man, whose name I will not give, but for the purpose of this story will call Ron, usually returned between twelve midnight and 1.00am. This night it was after 5.00am when he arrived at Chelmorton, and as he was staggering down Marston, he was met by a farmer going for his horse, ready to take the milk to the station.

Seeing Ron, covered in white road dust, the farmer ran up to him. *"Ron, where on earth have you been?"* He could see Ron's right arm was hanging limp *"What is the matter with you lad, have you been in an accident?"* but Ron could not speak. Getting hold of Ron's left arm, the farmer helped him back to the farm, the nearest household that was up and about. Sending his lad for the horse, the farmer and his wife tried to revive Ron, giving him hot, strong and sweet tea to drink and getting him warm.

When the lad had returned with the horse, the farmer went out, harnessed and put the horse into the shafts of the milk float (a light sprung cart) and loaded the milk churns ready for the station about two miles away. With everything ready to go, he went back into the house to see how Ron was doing. He looked a lot better but still had not said a word that could be understood.

"When I get to the station, I will send for Dr Hazlewood to come and set that broken arm", said the farmer. Off he went with the milk to the station where he went and found the Stationmaster to send for the doctor, while he unloaded the full churns and picked up empty ones ready for the next day. He then went back home as fast as he could, jumping out of the float and going straight back into the house to see how Ron was.

By now, Ron had come to his senses and told of his terrifying night. *"First I went to the Plough in Flagg for an odd tipple, just to quench my thirst, and then I moved on to the Bulls Head in Monyash for a drop more. I left there about 11.00pm and I walked up onto the Bakewell road and turned for Chelmorton. It was bright moonlight, I could see for miles, the road was like a white ribbon stretching over the hills* (the minor roads then were still metalled with broken limestone, ground to a white dust by the iron rims of cart and wagon wheels). *"*

"When I got to Thorn Pit (an old quarry owned by the Parish), *I heard a rumbling sound behind me and when I turned I saw a cloud of dust coming nearer and nearer. Out of the dust appeared six white horses galloping towards me, pulling a stagecoach. Now I knew that coaches have been gone for at least fifty years, and I just stood there, petrified, as it got nearer and nearer. It slowed down as it came close and it stopped right by my side. The coachman leaned over and said 'climb aboard', and reaching down he took hold of my right arm with a grip of iron which crushed it just as if it was in the jaws of a lion. He gave a horrible laugh, and then he let go of me and was gone in a cloud of dust. I saw the coach going straight on, even though the road divides after Thorn Pit* (Church Lane to the right, Marston to the left) - *it just appeared to go straight on where there has never has been a road."*

As he finished his story, a clatter of hooves heralded the arrival of Dr Hazlelwood. He had a quick look at Ron and said *"Load him into the milk cart and take him to the Cottage Hospital. He is suffering from severe shock as well as the broken arm. It looks as if it has been badly crushed in something."* With that he was outside, mounting his horse and away again.

Ron was helped into the milk float and taken to the Cottage Hospital. In spite of a lot of enquiries, there was never anything to suggest how he really got that crushed arm or how he had come to be in that state of shock or terror that he was in when he was found staggering down Marston by the farmer. One thing for certain, he never went that way again, even in daylight.

The story of Ron's coach spread like wild-fire round the villagers and much talk about ghosts and other weird goings-on was the height of conversation in the village inns for years to come. The tos and fros of all this story were being discussed one day in a village not far from Chelmorton, when one brave gentleman declared that there was no such thing as ghosts, and an argument broke out. But he stuck to his guns confidently.

Then one of the 'believers' threw out a challenge: *"You had better put your money where your mouth is - I bet you ten bob you dare not walk round the churchyard and then sit in the middle of it for half an hour."*

The 'unbeliever' jumped up straightway, pulling a ten bob note from his pocket, and giving it to Mr Needham, the landlord of the inn, to hold. The other man had to do likewise. He said, *"We will leave it nearer to midnight before the challenge is tried."* Some argument broke out over this, because the time then was only 9.00pm. With some of the customers having to be up at five, they wanted the bet over and done with. So a compromise of 10.30 was made - half way between nine and twelve midnight.

At about 10.15 pm, the believer said he would have to go - he had to be up early - and left his friend to time Len's brave visit to the churchyard.

At 10.30, Len was escorted to the churchyard gates. Quite unconcerned, he wandered across the dark churchyard to the accompaniment of hooting owls. But as he got to the far end of the churchyard, he heard a low moaning coming from a newly dug grave, ready for a funeral the next day. The gravedigger had left his spade standing up in the pile of newly dug earth, ready to tidy up any bits of earth that might drop off the sides during the night. As Len got nearer the moaning got louder. When he finally reached the spot and looked down into the open grave, he could see a white, ghostly figure lying in it. The moaning turned into eery words, *"It's cold down here, it's cold down here,"* whereupon Len, instead of running, grabbed the spade. *"No wonder you're cold,"* he said, *"they've forgotten to cover you up,"* and he started shovelling the soil into the grave. The moans suddenly changed to screams, *"It's only me, you silly b----r, stop trying to bury me."* Fortunately the so-called ghost's friends now came to his rescue.

Len won the ten bob with which he bought 20 pints of best Burton beer for everyone - and there was now another 'ghost story' to talk about in the pub!!

Two guineas please

Grandad used to tell us stories of Doctor Hazlewood who apparently was quite a character - there was no messing around with him. For instance, there was a man who thought himself a bit of a 'toff' and would not wait in the waiting room with us ordinary folk, but instead visited late, after all the 'rubbish' had gone. Even the good Doc did not like his attitude much, but he had money - and some of the smaller farmers and labourers had none.

On one particular day, the 'toff' limped into the surgery just as the Doctor was going out on his rounds. He was dressed in his riding gear and had his crop in his hand. *"What's the matter with you then?"* *"It's my big toe, it's gone septic."* *"Right, take off your slipper and put your foot on this stool,"* the Doctor said, pacing up and down the room, still dressed ready to go out. He used his riding crop the wrong way round, and kept tapping things around the room in his anger, while the patient got his slipper and extra large sock off. He got out a clean handkerchief, spread it over the stool so that his foot would not go where a 'commoner' had sat, then carefully placed his foot on it for the doctor to treat. Dr Hazelwood wandered over and took a look at the badly swollen toe which was all horrid and yellow. .

"Um," the doctor said, stroking his chin with his left hand, *"Umm, it is a bloody mess. Um, Um, it is, indeed."* Then, suddenly, he brought the riding crop over, like a hammer, and hit the offending toe a mighty whack with the handle. The toenail and matter flew in all directions. *"There,"* said the Doc, *"That will teach you to cut your bloody toe nails. That will be two guineas, please."* And off he went, leaving the patient to his own devices.

If, on his journeys, he ever came to a gate that was locked or a gate where there had not been one before, he would take a saw, which he carried in his saddle bag, and cut the obstructing gate or fence in two, or cut it completely down.

There were no bridle tracks closed when he was around as there are today. Even the Peak District National Park Authority has closed several to my own knowledge, with locks and chains.

Another familiar medical person was the midwife. One memorable occasion in the community was the time a local person tried to commit suicide for the sixth or seventh time, cutting his throat with a razor - deep but not deep enough to do much real harm and with a lot of blood flying around.

The relatives were unable to contact the doctor, so the midwife was hurriedly sent for. A big heavy lady, she arrived with what looked like a small bag- but it only looked small in her big fist. Putting it down on the floor she knelt down beside the patient. Seeing that no arteries or veins were cut she calmly got a darning needle and some good strong black thread out of the bag, threaded the needle, greased the thread with lard, then putting one knee firmly on the man's chest to hold him down, she proceeded to sew his throat up like a cotton bag. *"This will stop your suiciding!"* she said.

Anne Slack, local midwife.

Circus stunts

The Goulds lived at the Burrs for many years before us. Their parents died when they were young. Sally, the only daughter, was about 13, with two or three older brothers and one very young one. She did all the cooking and cleaning.

When they were collecting eggs, the older brothers used to come up from the hen coop (later made into a boar pen by Grandad) to the corner of the stable. When she went to the house door, they would throw the eggs for her to catch. If they threw too fast she would side-step them letting them go past to break against the fireplace or go into the ashpot underneath. When Grandad started to clear out the house, he got a barrow full of egg shells from under the fireplace.

There was a travelling circus showing at Buxton so the Gould troop marched off from the Burrs through Deep Dale to King Sterndale and then on to Buxton. Now amongst the acts was a young man standing on the far end of a plank over a barrel, while two heavier men jumped off a platform onto the other end, shooting the smaller man into the air to land on the shoulders of three other men already standing on each others' shoulders.

The following day, the Goulds got a long plank and, using the garden wall as a barrel, they took a 16 stone bag of flour upstairs and were about to drop it out onto the end of the plank with their younger brother on the other end. They were trying to shoot him up onto the house roof.

Luckily, a neighbour called to see them about that time, and, before they could drop the bag of flour onto the end of the plank, the neighbour grabbed the youngster and pulled him off the other end and so no harm was done.

Another Chelmorton farm, Shepley Farm

Reaping near the Burrs.

Sweet violets

A local story that one of our uncles told was about when Chelmorton had a very good man with a scythe. It was specially made for him by old George Smith when he was a young blacksmith. It was claimed that he could mow more in a day than anyone else around. A good scyther was always respected but this man was special.

It happened that Flagg had a good man as well, and after many arguments in the Church Inn and the Plough, it was decided to have a competition between them. Areas of land were carefully measured and marked out, and as it was going to be a weekend event, the local ladies of each village, supporting their own man, did the catering for the occasion. Chelmorton used a handy building for their catering, while Flagg borrowed a big tent from Flagg race committee.

But as Friday evening drew to a close, Flagg people got a bit nervous, wondering if their man would stand up to the job the next day. So to be sure they decided to put some wooden pegs in the Chelmorton plot; while some of the others did their part by adding some jollop into 'the Chelly mon's ale'!

Next morning, up bright and early with the sun, the men went to their posts and sharpened their scythes ready for the off. Now *the Chelly mon*, not feeling at all well in the tummy, tucked his trouser bottoms into his socks.

Someone started them off and in they went, scythes swinging purposefully. After a few minutes, '*the Chelly mon's* scythe hits a wooden peg, and putting extra effort into it he says, *"Oops a bloody dock!"* and looks a little uncomfortable'. And so it went on - each time he hit a peg, an extra bit of effort; and his trousers getting heavier each time! But never did he ease his pace.

And he won, but instead of going triumphantly to his own catering party on the Chelmorton side, he went straight to the Flagg tent - which he soon had to himself!

Tony Chapman.

Gweneth, Billy, Harry and Marion Swindell.

No money changed hands

Doctors were not always the best people to cure you in those days. There was one old gentleman near us who was crippled with some rheumatic ailment and needed two sticks to walk with. Grandad used to help him with his farm.

After some young cattle had been turned out into a twelve-acre field which had a mere in the middle of it, Grandad kept an eye on them, making sure that there was plenty of water in the mere. Because there was a young bull amongst them, he always carried a good stick and he knew how to use it. As he expected, one day, when he was visiting the mere, the bull decided it did not want anyone on his territory and set about shifting Grandad, coming at him with its head down, and tearing clods up with his front feet. With Grandad being young and agile and armed with a good stick, the bull had to retreat in the end. When he got back to the yard, he found the bull's owner and told  him not to go into the field where the bull was, because it had turned on him. *"Nowt of the sort, mon. It's only a bit of a calf, it'll do thee nou harm."* *"You will see,"* Grandad said. *"Keep away from him, I tell thee,"* and he then left his neighbour to make his own mind up.

A day or two later, Mr Wardle decided to go and look at the cattle himself. He went across to the gate and into the field with the bull in it, and had only gone about a hundred yards when the bull spotted him and charged, bellowing as it came thundering towards him. He threw down his sticks and ran for the gate, going faster and faster until he reached it, and jumping the gate just before the bull got there. He didn't need his walking sticks for a while after that!

A few years earlier, Dad, then between the age of nine and twelve, used to help Mr Wardle. One day, they had been sowing seeds with a horse and seed drill, with Dad leading the horse while the farmer looked after the drill. After going up and down the field about ten or twelve times, my Dad said, *"Have we got plenty of seed in the drill Mr Wardle?"* *"Yar, dunner yo bother abite sayd,"* he snapped, *"yo luk after th' tit!"* So Dad carried on leading the horse. After another half hour or so, Dad asked again about the seed - with the same sort of answer given. When the field was well on its way to being finished, the farmer eventually stopped and looked into the seed hopper. It was empty. Not knowing at what point the seed had run out, he did not know where to return to re-start the sowing. *"More haste, less speed Mr Wardle,"* Dad put in, at which the farmer exploded, unhooked the horse from the drill, and went home, taking the horse with him.

Shortly after they got back to the farm, Grandad, on his way home from working in the quarries, came to see if anything needed doing. *"Go wi Charlie and finish sowing them sayds,"* said the farmer. When Grandad and my Dad got into the fallow field Dad told him what had happened in the morning.

"Oh," said Grandad, *"We will soon sort that out."* After hooking the horse to the drill, they started at the other side of the field to the one where sowing began in the morning, making sure the drill seed hopper was full. They drilled up and down the field, just as in the morning, but Grandad kept an eye on the seed all the time, checking at the top of the field each time round. When the hopper was nearly empty, they stopped and counted how many rows had been done. It was found that one seed hopper full did fourteen rows with a bit to spare, so they now knew where the seed had run out in the morning - fourteen rows from the wall. So now, when they got to the last fourteen rows, they stopped, and went back to the farmyard.

"Are you sure you have sown em all?" asked the farmer. *"You will see for yourself in two or three weeks' time,"* said Grandad. *"And how many rows have you sown twice and will have seedling so thick they cannot grow? And how many will have no seed at all?"* he grumbled. *"Watch and wait, you will learn something,"* Grandad said. *"The proof of the sowing is in the growing."* After a month, when they looked at it again, all the field was growing level.

About six weeks later, this same farmer was mowing grass in a big meadow. He was constantly urging the horses to go faster till they were white with foaming sweat. The mower was going at a speed for which it was not intended and sooner or later something would give way. Suddenly the cutter bar hit a hidden mole heap. It ploughed through it, bending the connecting rod which was connected to the driven fly wheel at one end and the cutting knife at the other. As the flywheel was turning at 500 rpm, then the knife was moving backwards and forwards across the fingers at the same speed. This meant that the extra load on the knife as it went through the small heap of soil bent the connecting rod so the job had to stop. More haste, less speed again!

The farmer lifted the cutter bar, took the machine out of gear and drove the horses and mower over to the gateway where he stopped and called to Dad, who had to leave his job of raking out the backswathe. He went over to Mr Wardle and took the horses out of the mower shafts, letting them walk round the pasture field until they were cool, then through the gate and into the yard.

Meanwhile, Mr Wardle pulled the grass and soil from between the fingers of the machine, so as to free the knife and check it for damage. He dragged it out using a metal hook made for the job, then took off the bent connecting rod and went towards the main road, carrying the bent rod over his shoulder. Reaching the main road he walked to the bus stop, waited for two minutes, then impatience overcame him and he set off to walk to Buxton. He had not gone very far when the bus overtook him, but eventually he got to the blacksmith's shop and handed over the bent connecting rod to be straightened.

The blacksmith placed the rod across the anvil, took up a hammer, and gave it a couple of hits. He then took up the rod and looked along it from end to end, put it back onto the anvil and gave it a couple more taps. He looked at it again, gave it one more tap and then said, *"There Mr Wardle, I think it's all right now"*, whereupon the farmer snatched it off the blacksmith; *"I could have done that blessed much fer mesel,"* he said, and marched off in a temper. With it being ten minutes before a bus was due, he set off walking all the way back. He hadn't walked the first mile before the bus overtook him. But that was how he was, always in a rush and getting nowhere fast.

The other side of him was kindness itself. Grandad could have as many swedes as he wanted throughout the winter. He could grow two or three rows of potatoes, enough to keep them all year round providing we set them and weeded them. But the land was already ploughed, cultivated, mucked and rowed up and at harvest time, the farmer would lend him a horse, cart, bags and plough to split the rows, so potatoes could be picked easily. He also let Grandad keep two lots of hens on his land and gave him four pints of milk a day. This was all for the little help for which Grandad could spare the time - no money ever changed hands! The custom still goes on today. A lot of country people have two accounts, one in a bank and one in goodwill - the latter being the most valuable.

Have you seen anything of my Dad?

In 1936 Dad decided to do some repairs to the calf-shed roof. He got the gear together, including, slates, repair tools and a ladder. He climbed up onto the roof, then moved upwards to the offending hole in the slates. He started working on the slates around the hole but the roof was wet and because the branch of a sycamore tree hung over it, there was a fine green moss growing on the slates. Suddenly, he slipped and slid down the roof, falling heavily onto his back in the stone yard.

Although he was suffering with pain, he got up and after a while went and fetched a cart rope. He threw it over the roof, fastened it to a stone drinking trough, then went up onto the roof again, fastening himself to the rope so that he could not slip again, and he finished repairing the leaking roof.

It was a week before Dad was fit for work again. He did piecework at Blackwell Mill Quarries where he filled stone for fivepence a ton. He averaged six pounds a week and so he must have filled 120 tons a week. This stone had to be broken down to a set size, using a 27lb hammer.

On the first Saturday in December 1937, Dad took Ma to Buxton in the afternoon with his motorbike and sidecar, to do some shopping. As it was beginning to snow hard and all the provisions for winter had not yet been bought we knew it would be late when they got back. I did all the farm jobs before it got dark, except for milking the cow. I took two buckets of coal into the house, a bag of logs and the sticks for the fire lighting the following morning. With all the outside work done and the door closed and bagged up (a folded bag placed across the bottom of the door to stop draughts), we settled down to wait for Dad to return.

Five o'clock; shouldn't be long now, I assured my two little sisters. Six o'clock came and there was still no sign of our parents. I was getting worried. They had never been this late before. At about 6.30, I made a drink and some sandwiches to pass the time, as we were getting hungry. At seven o'clock, as no more snow had fallen during the day, I knew it was not this that was causing the trouble. They must have broken down.

Other farmers also went to Buxton on a Saturday, with it being Market

Day, so if they had broken down someone would give them a lift. They would have gone home first to unload their day's shopping and then they would bring Dad and Mum down here to the Burrs later. By eight o'clock, Muriel and Joyce had gone to bed. On one of the many times I went outside to look and listen for them, I unchained Prince, Dad's black and tan collie and brought her into the house with me for company. She would hear them from further afield than I could and would tell me of their approach by her movements and whines. We had four dogs called Prince over the years - always Prince - and they were all bitches!

Eight-thirty and still nothing. Dad must be helping whoever had given them a lift to milk and feed their cows before being brought home, if indeed they had broken down and if they had been offered a lift. Too many ifs, I was beginning to think. Nine o'clock; still nothing.

I put the kettle back on the fire to boil so I could make myself a mug of cocoa, when suddenly Prince's ears began to move. She was listening very intently and then she moved towards the door. By her actions, I knew there was something, or someone about, but certainly not my Dad. She began to growl, looking at me to make sure I was aware of what she had heard. Her bite was worse than her bark, for she had been trained not to bark if you were with her.

By the direction of her head and ears I knew someone was coming across the little meadow towards the stile into the well yard, so I went into the dark kitchen to look through the small window. Sure enough, a figure came over the stile into the well yard and round the mere towards the door. I could not see who it was but, knowing where the path was, it must be a friend and Prince was not too aggressive, even when a knock came on the door. A voice, which I had heard before, said *"It's Eddie. Are you all right?"*

By now, both Prince and I had relaxed so I moved the bag from the door, opened it and Eddie Bosley came in, closing the door behind him. *"Have you seen anything of my Dad?"* I asked him. *"No,"* he said, *"but there has been an accident and your Dad has been taken to hospital. Your Ma is there with him. She is not hurt but has to stay there until tomorrow. She telephoned the Post Office, the only telephone in the village, to let Mrs Hawley know what had happened so someone would come and see if you children were OK".*

I thanked him for walking all the long way down to the Burrs to see that we were all right and made him a hot drink, saying we were getting short of milk until the cow was milked. *"Who milks her then?"* he asked. *"My Dad is the only one who can milk her. She kicks a bit, so I leave her alone. I have fed her but that is all".*

Mr Bosley finished his drink and then said, *"Let's have a look at this milk cow and see if I can milk her for you".* I got him the clean milk bucket out of the pantry and off he went into the shippon. He looked at the cow, talking to her all the time. Then he got a milk stool while I gave her a scoop of corn. He cleaned her udder, sat himself down and started to milk her. After one minute, she tried to kick him out but he held her firm and finished the job of milking, pulling the stool away.

We took a half bucket of milk into the house for me to sieve and leave to cool. Mission completed, Eddie went home the way he had come. At about 11 o'clock, I gave Prince a dish of the warm milk, let her out for a run round, then kept her in the house for the rest of the night. I did not go to bed but slept on the sofa after banking up the fire to last all night.

The next morning, after my sisters got up, I made some bread and milk for us, including Prince, then I went out to feed the animals. Muriel and Joyce went to let the hens out and feed them for me. All this took about an hour after which we were ready for a proper breakfast. I had told my sisters that Mum and Dad would be back later; that was all. We managed to make some breakfast. When Eddie returned, he had a drink and a bacon sandwich with us. *"By gow, you're managing well, young Claude,"* he said. *"I better milk that grumpy cow of yours again."* But before he milked her, he got the barrow and shovel and cleaned all the cows out. I was really glad of this, because it was a very heavy job for me.

When he had done all he could do and was just getting ready to go home, Mr Grindey arrived on his usual Sunday morning visit. *"Have you heard owt about how Charles is, Tom?"* Eddie asked. He said he had but then they had a quiet talk on their own. *"I'll have to be going now then, young man,"* said

Eddie, *"but I'll be back t'night to milk the cow and see what's happening."*

Mr Grindey came into the house, sat down and had a talk to us. He asked if we were going to Sunday School, which we usually did on a Sunday morning. I told him that we wouldn't be going as Dad and Ma might come back at any time. *"What are you going to do about dinner?"* he said, *"You can all come home with me for dinner if you like."* *"Thank you very much, Mr Grindey, but we will be alright, thanks. I'd rather wait for Ma and Dad."* *"I suppose you will at that,"* he replied, *"Is there owt you need doing before I go."* I told him that I thought everything was all right for now and thanked him again.

Just then we heard a car coming along the Top Lane, and after a few minutes it appeared at the top of the stable field but did not come any further, with the snow lying deep in the bottom stable field. It was young Sam Bagshaw and he had brought Ma home. We all ran up the field to meet Ma. *"How's Dad"* I asked. *"Oh, he'll be alright but he'll have to stay in hospital a few days."*

We all carried the shopping down to the house between us. Mr Grindey had watched from the yard and when he saw it was Ma, he went into the house and got the kettle to fill with water from the churn outside the door. He took it in to boil on the fire, so that Ma could have a hot drink when she came in.

As soon as the bags of groceries were into the house, and Ma had had a pot of tea, she sent us round the hen coops to collect eggs to give to Mr Grindey to take back to Chelmorton for Mrs Hawley, for alerting the village to the accident. While we were out she told Mr Grindey how bad Dad really was. He was still unconscious and she did not expect him home for a long time!

During the next few weeks, everyone in the village did what they could for us, especially Mr Eddie Bosley, for whom we had never yet done anything ourselves. He walked to the Burrs every night and morning, before

and after going to work, to milk the cow and do anything else heavy that needed doing.

Soon after Dad's accident I learned to milk. I managed to milk the cow at one end of the day, with Mr Bosley coming to milk her properly at the other end. After a few further weeks I milked her both night and morning - letting myself in for a job for some years to come, including the trick of holding cows with my left arm, preventing me from being kicked out from underneath them.

Mr Grindey brought drinking water with his horse and cart. It was a good job we already had plenty of coal and firewood in for the winter.

Mr Chapman took Ma to see Dad several times a week. I think he was in hospital for seven or eight weeks. I know it was a very bad Christmas for us in spite of the kindness of the village people who offered us hospitality in their homes. Eventually Dad came home but he was not able to do anything and he suffered from very bad headaches and was very short tempered. He was never really the same again.

Alan Sellers, Jimmy Mellor, Colin Goodwin and Sydney Bagshaw.

Mavis.

Last of the Summer Wine! Mr Bagshaw, Mr Grindey and Mr Solomon (Sol) Mellor.

Good Neighbours

We were very fortunate in the richness of heaven sent friends, from the gypsies who wandered in and out of our lives, to local dignitaries. I do not know how to list them, they were all so dear to my family. I will start with Cllr. Sam Swindell. He was the person we turned to when we needed good letters writing.

Sam Swindell

His letters were like a solicitor's, and made a big difference to Dad winning his case against the owners of the wagon which caused the accident. He also wrote the successful letter applying for the tenancy of the Bagshawe Arms Inn and Farm.

In fact we turned to Shepley farm for so many things. When we went to see Mr and Mrs Swindell, we not only got good advice, but good hospitality as well. Always a cheerful welcome, a cup of tea and homemade cake, or pastry, to discuss business over. I can still

Harry Swindell

Colin Goodwin

remember their big iron kettle singing a special song of its own. When placed nearer the fire its tune changed, coming up to a peak just as it came to boiling point.

During the season Mrs Swindell would take me into her flower garden; the scent of all those blooms was overpowering. She would wander from place to place, picking as she went, until she had a nice bunch, then she gave them to me to take home to my mother. Later on in life Mr Swindell was awarded the MBE for his services to the community.

Harry Swindell and his Shorthorn bull.

There were many other good neighbours like those already mentioned - the Grindeys, the Chapmans, the Bagshaws -and many others.

Before motorised transport livestock had to be moved by horse and cart, or driven on foot along lanes, packhorse trails or bridleways. With cows being much larger than pigs and sheep they were nearly always driven on foot. In those days it was only the large farms that kept a bull. When we had a cow that needed mating we would drive her to Mr Swindell's bull at Shepley Farm. They always kept a good pedigree Shorthorn bull.

Now driving one cow is hard work. It is much easier to drive a herd once they get going and a lead cow has taken over. It is still a mystery to me how they sort themselves out. The order of march is the medium cows in front, then the best fighters, followed by the old, then the cows with calves.

An easy move is about ten miles per day, letting them graze along the way. Watering places are always important of course.

I was glad to be back

Negligence was proven against the driver of the wagon which hit my Dad and he was awarded £1,250. When he was able to get around, he used some of this to buy a very good horse from a farm sale. When we bought the horse, as we were taking her out of her stable, the wife of the farmer we had bought the horse from was crying. *"You'll look after Bess for me won't you? She has never once been hit by hand or stick and, in return, she has never kicked, bitten or harmed anyone".* She said a tearful goodbye to Bess and left us to it.

All the time we had Bess, she was never hit or ill used in any shape or form. She was a lady of high standing, a willing worker and when she was loose in a field, all you had to do if you wanted her for work, was to go to the gate and call her name. She would come straight over to you. Stella was very jealous of the new competition and when she had to do a little work, she stopped playing lame.

Harold Mellor.

After a year or two she was sired by a pedigree shire and had a filly foal we called Phyllis, a fine chestnut with four white socks. She took after her Mum, a lovely horse and a kind and a willing worker.

With Bess and a good cart, Dad was able to get around to other farm sales easily and this gave him a fresh interest in life. When he had got some farm implements together, he started looking for a farm near to a school so we wouldn't have to walk as far, and where there was water laid on, so there was no more carting. The only one in his range which met the requirements was an eighty-acre farm in Wormhill called the Bagshawe Arms, which had the village inn with it.

Inn or not, Dad decided to go for it. After several days had elapsed, an old lady came to the Burrs and said that she had it on good authority that we were

My Dad at the Burrs.

The Bagshawe Arms at Wormhill.

hoping to leave - and had the place been let or sold. We asked her in. She sat on a chair next to the table, her eyes everywhere. She remarked on the quality and age of some of the furniture we had, and Ma and the visitor talked for some while as to the history of certain pieces. The fact was my great grandparents had worked at Alton Towers in service and were married from there. Some surplus furniture had been presented to them as a wedding present. After she had eaten her fill of pastries and drank her tea, she bid us good day, not before remarking how beautiful the place was, and to ask why were we leaving. Ma told her to be nearer to a school for her young daughters, and to have water coming out of a tap for the first time in their lives! She smiled and was gone, walking up the fields to the road.

After two days a letter arrived from the Bagshawe estate saying we had got the tenancy of the Bagshawe Arms from the 25th March 1939. Signed Mrs. B.M.W. Bagshawe, with a footnote, *"thank you for the refreshments and the interesting talk at the Burrs farm."*

It was now about the last week in January, so we only had eight weeks to get our gear together, apply for a licence for the inn, as well as a thousand and one other jobs to do. At first, I was excited about moving but then I began to change my mind. The thought of leaving the Burrs with all its wildlife and the dales, which I had come to know inside out, to go to a place I did not know. It was too much. So Dad, in his wisdom, said he would take me to look at the place.

One Saturday morning, we harnessed Bess, put her in the cart and off we went, armed with sandwiches and a bottle of tea each, up the stable fields, onto the top lane and on to Coalpit Lane, up over Colton and down to the Buxton-Bakewell road. We turned right for 200 yards, then left down the twisting road to Miller's Dale, left again and up and under two low railway bridges and on up to Wormhill.

It was a nasty, drizzly day, with the fine rain collecting on the branches of the trees and falling in big drops. There were trees, trees, everywhere and the place looked miserable and cold. I was not impressed. There was mud on the road from the wheels of muck carts, while others carted hay in from stacks in the field - making an even worse mess because they came off the land heavily loaded up. Going up Wormhill Cutting was particularly grim, with the road going up between two steep banks and the trees dripping on us.

The village itself was better. There were no overhanging trees here and we went past the one and only shop-cum-post-office with the phone box outside. We went on past Brindley Well, put up in honour of James Brindley, the canal and waterways engineer born in Wormhill. One hundred yards further - and there was the Bagshawe Arms. There were two gateways into it, one for the farm and one for the inn but the broken limestone drives and the yard formed a horseshoe, so you could go in at one gate and out the other.

The farm buildings for cows were on your right with the big, very good stable in front of you and the inn and farmhouse to the left. If you went in through the top gate these would be straight in front of you, with a three-foot dry limestone wall on your left and what was left of Wormhill Village Green. In the middle of the two drives and yard there was a water supply laid on, but there was no electric or telephone, just paraffin lamps.

The school was only two hundred yards away and you did not even have to cross a road to get to it. *"That's handy,'* I thought doubtfully, *"they can watch and make sure I get to school."*

The journey back to The Burrs was uneventful. Going down the stable field, I thought how welcoming it looked, not at all like the Bagshawe Arms. I was very glad to be back.

Wormhill stocks.

Ready for the road

In the following weeks, Dad and Bess went to a lot of farm sales, buying what would be needed for the bigger farm. He was always on the lookout for machines and tools that were cheap, even if they needed repairing, which we did at night. Neighbours lent us two drays which we slowly began to load with all manner of things, ready to flit to Wormhill on March 25th. Uncle Mo came each Sunday to help, bringing with him my cousin George. In the last days before the move, George and I talked a lot about the Bagshawe Arms, although he had not yet seen it himself.

Ma did a lot of baking, enough to see us, as well as all the helpers, fed during the move. The nearer the day loomed, the more I hated the idea of leaving The Burrs. I begged my Dad to buy the Burrs off Grandad and stay there. He said he had already tried that, but Grandad would not sell it to us and with the threat of war hanging over us, all the farms were being snapped up by people from the towns and cities, with a lot more money than country folk, so it was a case of take what you could find.

Even in an isolated place like The Burrs, we knew, from the wireless and second-hand newspapers, that war was coming. Not only that; we could see it for ourselves. As early as 1937, strange beams of light had begun to appear in the night sky. To begin with, there were only three or four, but as the weeks passed by, more came to join them until there must have been twenty-five to thirty. It was hard to count them because they kept switching on and off in a random fashion. When one switched on, another would go off, but I noticed the base of light went out first, leaving the beam of light to roll up into the clouds and then when another was switched on, the base came on, then quickly the beam shot up into the sky. I was witnessing the speed of light I suppose. I could not understand what was really happening. The only thing to do was to ask.

The first person I saw was Mr Gould coming down the little lane. As he got over the stile into our little meadow at the bottom of the lane, I went to meet him on the path which goes past the Burrs. I could see he was in a hurry, so when he got near enough, I quickly bid him *"Good morning"* and quickly asked about the lights.

"Oh," he said, *"I am in a hurry. I will stop and talk to you later"*. And he was gone down the path towards the quarry where he worked. I did my last jobs, went into the house, got changed into my school clothes and then Muriel and I were off to school for the day. As soon as that long, boring day was over and we were dismissed, I was out of the door, across to Mr Grindey's to get water and by then Muriel had come out and was waiting for me. We got home in less than half an hour that night.

I changed into my work clothes, fed the hens and collected the eggs from all those places way off the yard, so as to be close at hand when Mr Gould came up from the quarry. The eggs I had collected were taken off me by Ma to wash and put away in the very cool pantry. I relaxed and got on with jobs in the yard.

At about 5.00pm Mr Gould appeared up the footpath, tired and dusty. I thought to myself, *"He will not want to talk tonight, he will want to get home."* But to my surprise he said, *"Hello, Claude, do you think your mother will have the kettle on?"* *"Yes,"* I answered, with delight, taking my guest into the house, where he sat down on a strong chair.

Mother soon fixed him up with a mug of tea and a plate with cake and pastry on. I waited for him to say something about the lights, but no, he just ate and congratulated Ma on her baking. Then, to my surprise, he said that he used to live here when he was a boy. He knew all the secret hiding places - like the priest hole and other things I thought only I knew.

Then he said, *"These lights you have been seeing at night. The army is responsible. They are learning to catch enemy bombers in their beam to give anti-aircraft gunners a chance to shoot them down. Now that is done by teamwork. When one light catches an aircraft in its beam, others swing onto it. Three or four form a box. It is very hard to get out of these blinding lights and the guns can zero in on the enemy. When searchlights and guns are in groups, they are called batteries. They work very well together with practice and that's just what they are doing."* He thanked Ma for the brew and cake, and then was gone up the path towards Chelly.

Throughout 1938, the night sky continued to be lit up to the west by searchlight beams, criss-crossing and piercing the night sky, searching for the target aircraft. When one beam picked it out, the others would immediately swing their beam onto it from other angles, thus forming a box of light giving the anti-aircraft guns a clear target.

By day, other old and slow aircraft flew around, obviously as day targets for gunners and observers. On one windy day, an escaped barrage balloon sailed over. We were to see many more of these in the early 1940s. They were very dangerous for they were dragging their long, steel mooring lines behind them and as these were being dragged over high voltage electric cables, everything they touched, like metal roofs, buildings, telephone wires, became live. This was the main danger.

The Territorial Army training intensified. One of our friends, Billy Hewitt, who had been in the RAF, was re-called to duty. The land of Britain was like a farm getting ready for winter, I thought. People in the towns had seen the news at the cinemas, had seen what had happened to the Spanish towns under aerial bombardment and if, and when, war broke out, they expected the same to happen to them, so a lot of people, who could, got out into the country while they could. Some even sent their children out of the way to Canada and America and people from Europe, especially Jews, began to arrive in this country to be safer. The lucky ones, that is.

Ma had got together a very large stock of tinned food, sugar and other long keeping foodstuff such as tea, coffee and cocoa. Farmers were quietly buying stocks of ammunition for any firearms they had. Not that invasion was on anyone's mind, but, if war broke out, this sort of thing would be very hard to get hold of. Even if the government of the day were not really preparing for war, in case of upsetting Hitler, the country folk were doing the best they could to be ready.

On the 15th March, Dad began taking the implements to Wormhill. First he took the swathe turner. He did not know how Bess would act with the noise of the iron-wheeled swathe-turner behind her on the road. After grooming Bess until she shone jet black, we harnessed her and put her into the shafts of the turner. When Dad was ready for off, he said, *"Nip up and open the top gate for me and stay there for a few minutes after we have gone through, because if she is very upset by the noise, I will come back with her"*. Away I went up the two fields to open the gate and hold it back while Dad and Bess went through onto the lane. As soon as the iron wheels left the grass and went onto the stone lane, the noise started but Bess took no notice of it at all. As they passed out of sight along the lane, I closed the gate and went back to do my jobs.

Dad arrived back about four hours later, with a handy cart that Mr Jack Wild from the post office farm had loaned him for a week or two. Tied to the back of the cart, was a light, handy horse about fifteen hands, for me to drive, Dad said. *"What's his name, Dad?"* *"Jack, "* he replied. *"He is very quiet. Untie him now from the cart and look after him with a drink and a bit of good hay."* *"What breed is he, Dad?"* I asked. *"A Dales I think,"* he told me, as he unharnessed Bess and rubbed her down.

Ma came out of the house now with three carrots. The first one she took over to Stella who was looking on suspiciously, leaning over the garden field wall; the next was to Bess, and the last one to Jack. We always tried to keep feeding in order of seniority. Stella had been at the Burrs the longest, so she was still top horse on this farm.

That night Dad sorted out some loads fit for Jack and me, ready for next morning. I was up very early, full of excitement, I got all my jobs done quickly, went to Bess, put a halter on her neck and led her into the yard, and tied her to a ring in the stable wall. I now took another halter to fetch Jack but he did not want to be caught. OK, I knew what to do; I went back for a bucket with a handful of corn in the bottom and tried again, and this time he soon came to me. When he had his head in the bucket, I got hold of his mane so I could hold him. When he pulled his head out of the bucket, I put the halter on him and he was no trouble at all after that.

Now I had hold of him, I took him to the yard and tied him up like Bess.

After breakfast, I gave him a good brushing down, which he obviously enjoyed, then after we had geared up Bess, we put Jack into the shafts of the handy cart, and Bess into

the raking machine. We were ready for off! Dad said to me, *"Now then, young man, I think it'll be best to go and open top gate and fasten it open, then come back for the horse and cart and follow me."*

By the time Jack and I got to the top gate, Dad had stopped, with the wide raking machine blocking the gateway. He watched us come up the field, saw that the job was going well and that I had control of Jack and drove off towards Wormhill, with me following with the cart, empty except for a basket of sandwiches, tea - and of course four carrots for Bess and Jack.

It was a clear, crisp morning, much better than the last time I went to Wormhill with Dad. The horses were going well and things looked a lot better from my little cart. The village, as we approached, also looked far better than last time, and I began to think it might be alright after all.

When we got to the Bagshawe Arms, Dad told me to stop in the yard with Jack while he took the raking machine and parked it in the orchard. Orchard! It was a croft the same size as a football pitch with elm, beech and sycamore growing round the wall sides.

Whilst Dad was taking Bess out of the machine, Eric Wainwright came up to me to talk, and he was asking a lot of questions but, for answer, only received further questions. *"How many cows do you have?"* *"One or two"* I said. *"What about horses?"* *"Two."* *"Will they work and can you catch them when you want them?"* *"How many fields have you? Where do you come from? Are all the gaps built up round the fields? How much was the rent? Are you going to buy or rent this farm? How much have you made off the place you have come from?"* I mainly dodged his questions. *"We have not sold it and we are not going to."* I said. I did not want to tell him Grandad owned it - I let him think what he wanted. And with that, in the end, he gave up.

Dad came back into the yard with Bess. *"I've had a word or two with Eric."* he said. Then we put the harness in my cart, tied Bess on behind and set off back for The Burrs. *"What do you think of the place now,"* he said, as we left Wormhill behind us. *"It seems a lot better this time, Dad,"* I said.

Just over the river bridge at Miller's Dale we stopped on a wide grass lay-by, had our sandwiches, gave the horses the carrots, and took Jack out of the shafts. I unharnessed him while Dad harnessed Bess and put her into them instead. It was Jack's turn to be tied behind. Back in the cart, a signal on the reins and we were off up the hill, heading for The Burrs again. Jack and the light cart now made Dad's ferrying problems easy. He could not walk far after the accident, so this was a good solution.

We were back about one, and we rubbed the horses down before we turned them out to graze after a feed of hay. After dinner, I went and caught old Stella. She had not worked for some weeks and immediately the harness went on, she went lame - and lamer still when put in the cart. I got some tools into the cart and went to an empty hen coop in the fallow field. We tied Stella to the gate - if we had not, whether lame or not, she would have soon bolted, if only to show off in front of the other two horses. We set about dismantling the hencoop and loading it onto the cart, roof panels, then sides and the floor panels last. If you can, it is always best to load ready to unload in the right order to re-assemble. The panels were bolted together, so they came to pieces very easily.

In less than an hour we were heading back to the yard. *"That's loaded for morning"*, Dad said, happily. He was ready for the road. He called it a day and we went in to listen to Inspector Thornley of Scotland Yard on the wireless. Just as it finished, the accumulator went flat, and the sound slowly died away - that would be it until we got to Wormhill, where we could get them re-charged on the spot, instead of having to walk a mile each way to Chelmorton - Wormhill was looking more attractive by the moment!

The next morning, off we went as before, Dad in front with Bess, now pulling the tedding machine. Jack had a load on his cart, but it made little difference to him, because he was a very powerful little horse. In Wormhill Dad parked the tedder in line with the other machines in the orchard, before we led both horses into a croft through the next gateway, where we chose a site to unload and rebuild the hen coop, ready to put the hens straight into.

Back at the Burrs again, the horses unharnessed, rubbed down, fed and turned out, we had dinner before we went and found some crates. We packed them into the cart along with the tools, and caught Stella, lame again, to take the cart up to the coop in the top stable field where I called the hens. It was feeding time, but I made a line of the corn through the entry tunnel into the coop, which they followed, one after another, 'til they were all inside. With Stella securely tied to the tree, we got the crates ready. I went inside the coop, caught the hens and passed them out to Dad, who put them into the waiting crates. We dismantled and loaded the coop as before, and then placed the crates of hens on top. Back in the Burrs yard we loaded the crates into our home-made cart. We loosed Stella, and she snorted and galloped away, with no sign of a limp.

The next day we took a cart each. We let the crated hens out in the Croft and left them with food and water until we had re-built the second coop. All was now ready for the big move, and we went to Mr Wilds to give him his cart back. Dad thanked him warmly, before we set off home with Jack in tow behind. The next job was going to be the move in six days' time.

Sitting on the silage clamp

Buxton House Mere and farmyard looking towards Meadow Place.

Buxton House Mere looking towards Buxton House Farm.

Last days at the Burrs, 1939

We used the last few days to get everything ready for loading. We didn't know how many horses and carts there would be turning up to help us move. On the morning of the 25th, the first to turn up was Uncle Mo with a pair of shires and a four-wheeled dray from Morton's at Cowdale. Next came Mr Mellor with two more shires and a heavy cart; then John and Henry Rains with a pair of Clydesdales. Now Harry Swindell with one shire and a skewbald Irish draught, and Uncle Norman with two shires. So with our two horses that made twelve horses altogether.

The horses were all groomed and harnessed up to show standard, while the men were all well turned out with highly polished leggings. What a wonderful sight it was. We loaded up and formed a convoy, moving off up the stable field and out onto the lane and away towards Wormhill.

When we got onto Wormhill Flatts, before Chapel Steads, we rested the horses. Before we set off again, we checked our spacing to about ten paces between each vehicle and we moved off again up into the village. The sound of the horseshoes ringing, as we climbed up through Wormhill cutting, is something I will never forget. I think all Wormhill turned out to watch us move. It was like a circus show with the skewbald leading.

Cousin George and I had made special plans for when we got to Wormhill; we had stowed away a pint pot each. When we pulled up and people were busy unloading, we sneaked down into the cellar where there was a row of barrels. I turned a tap on one and it came out under pressure, hit the bottom of the pot and splashed out again towards the ceiling. I switched the tap off quickly, but George was doing quite alright with another one that ran slowly. We got about half a pint each of this.

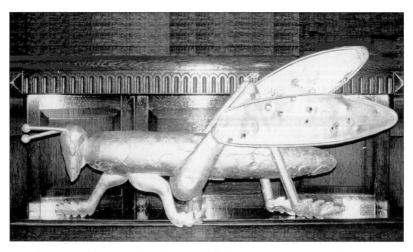

Locust weather vane from the top of Chelmorton church, down for repairs.

George took a drink out of his and said it was very good. So I took a gulp. I thought it was awful, but didn't say so because I didn't know what beer should taste like. So we drank some more. After a while the room appeared to be going round and I felt very poorly. We later found out that the beer we had been drinking had been condemned and had been waiting to go back to the brewery since Christmas. It put me off drinking beer for the rest of my life!

Mum and Muriel with help from others, had been busy getting the house in order. Licensing hours were eleven till three then but we had to take over at midday, and the Excise Officer turned up to check the legal side of the business; like the measures and specific gravity of the spirits.

Muriel remembers mostly being surprised at the people coming into the pub through more than one door - there were three entrances. We were only used to the one doorway at the Burrs.

A good home

Dad asked Mr Taylor, who went to cattle markets every week, to see if he could find about ten newly calved heifers for him, and sure enough, about a week later, a cattle wagon arrived with ten heifers which were unloaded into the big shippon.

Dad asked how much they were. *"I'll show you,"* Mr Taylor said, pulling some receipts from his inside pocket and showing Dad what they had cost at the market at Haslingden. They had cost £23 each plus £10 carriage. Dad asked Mr Taylor how much he wanted for his costs. Mr Taylor immediately replied, *"Nothing, I'm all right with the bit of luck money the vendors gave me."*

Luck money is a custom among farmers. If you charge a farmer for something and he pays in cash, he will usually ask for some luck, meaning some discount. Dad was very pleased and he gave Mr Taylor his £240. Then he sent me to the house for a bottle of Old Angus, the label of which had a picture of an old shepherd holding a lamb on it. I returned, holding it very carefully. That bottle meant more to Mr Taylor than money. He received money from many places, and it did not mean much to him; as he said, *"You can't eat or drink pound notes"*.

The cows began to settle down at the end of their long day. They had been loaded early in the morning and taken to the cattle market, before being driven from the holding pens into the sale ring, then driven again by men with sticks round the ring as the bidding started. The auctioneer would have brought his short stick down with a bang on his desk, *"Sold to Mr Taylor of Wormhill"*. The cows were driven out of the ring again, into more holding pens, before being loaded to come to us.

These ten cows were lucky - they had come to a good home. There would be no more markets for them, all being well, although one of them that we could not get in calf was sold after about twelve months. The nine that we kept for years were Curly, White Socks, Daisy, June, Mavis, Gwen, Joan, Brindle and Clara. After more than fifty years I can even remember where and in which order they were tied when in the shippon.

The next performance was milking them all by hand. There were no machines on small farms in those days. Dad milked Curly first, who was very hard to milk and kicked. Next came White Socks. She did not kick and was easy to milk, and Daisy was the same. June was nasty to begin with but soon settled down. Now Mavis was perfect. After Dad had milked her the first time

Unloading the hay at the Bagshawe Arms.

REDUCED PRICE LIST.

JOHN COOKE & SONS, Ltd.,

LINCOLN

SEPTEMBER 1st, 1933.

N.B.—All new Ploughs &c. are sent Carriage Paid; plough fittings to the value of £4 are sent carriage paid to English and Welsh Stations and to Scotch and Irish Stations to the value of £5.

ANGLE IRON AND WOOD BEAM PLOUGHS.

Page in Catalogue.	Mark.	No Wheels. £ s. d.	Two Wheels. £ s. d.	Steel Breast.	Skim Coulter.
3	XL 2 ...	7 19 0	9 15 0	... 4/6 ...	10/6
3	XL 1 ...	7 15 0	9 8 0	... 4/6 ...	10/6
3	XLRC	5 18 6	7 7 0	... 4/6 ...	10/6
4	XLRC No. 2	7 14 0	9 10 0	Included	10/6
5	XLSS ...	8 5 0	10 0 0	Included	10/6
5	XLSS ...(Long with all match appliances)		11 9 0	Included	
5	XLSS (Short ditto)		10 18 0	Included	
5	XLSS (Long & Short do.)		12 7 0	Included	

COOKE'S
CELEBRATED
AGRICULTURAL WAGONS.

For Farm and Road Work, and General Purposes.

COOKE'S
NEWLY-IMPROVED
COMBINED CART and WAGON.

A perfect Cart, and as useful as a Wagon for harvesting, &c., &c.

I would milk her afterwards. Gwen turned out to be a villain and needed a strong hand, Joan was very lively, Brindle very quiet and a good milker, but Clara had a mind of her own. When she was good, she was very, very good, but when the mood took her, she would try to kick you, the bucket, and the stool, right through the window. Anything could set her off. She was the last to be milked in the row and if the water you used to wash the udder had gone cold by the time you milked her, she would suddenly kick with both back legs at once, sending you, bucket, milk and stool flying. If you hit her for something, she would remember it, not kicking anyone else in the meantime, until you tried to milk her again. Cows have got long memories. Well, she damned well had!

There was a lot more work now. Pigs and hens still needed feeding and cleaning out, cows had to be milked and generally looked after, there was muck carting and spreading, walls to be built, gates and gateways to be repaired. At about 7.00 am I would go out and load the manure from the cows into a barrow and take it out to the muck heap, then clean the cows' trough and make ready to give them corn. Dad would bring the milk buckets and a bucket of warm, soapy water with a cloth in it to wash the cows' udders. Now Dad would give the first cow (Curly) her corn while I washed her bag, then Dad sat down and milked her. I moved on to White Socks giving her corn and cleaning her bag. Cleaning, corning and milking took four to five minutes per cow with good teamwork. When Curly was milked, Dad tipped the warm milk into one of the other buckets, then added White Socks' milk to another and would carry these two to the dairy. Standing on a box, I would tip them one at a time through the sieve into the tank above the cooler. The cooler was about 2ft square by 3ins thick, and there was a corrugated hollow section through which the cold water ran. The warm milk flowed down the outside of the section becoming cold as it reached the bottom and into the churn. When each churn was full it was moved and an empty one put in its place.

When all the milking. sieving and cooling was done, the full churns were measured and labelled ready for the milk wagon to take them into the city for the milk men to deliver in handy bottles.

During the first few weeks we started to produce milk for sale, Mr Beal from Rowsley would collect it. He had a shop at one of the junctions of the A6 which was very handy for outlying farms from different directions. In his wagon cab he carried a long box of tobacco, sweets and newspapers and he was a daily contact with the outside world for many small farms. Other milk wagons also collected from our area, and there was great competition amongst them to get the most lucrative farms for themselves. The farms close to the road sold the most milk and had it ready for collection early in the morning, which meant the owner-drivers had to be on the road very early.

The King of the Road, in those ruthless days of 'eat or be eaten', was George Bull. He had a load of milk on its way to the dairy in Sheffield before some of the others had started. After he had done his milk run, he would unload the empty churns, return, re-load and use the wagon for any other haulage he could get for the remainder of the day, and indeed half the night, trying to make enough money to buy his own farm. And he did, as well as an inn and a fleet of coaches! But with war looming, the system was soon to change and collecting areas were zoned to keep mileage down to a minimum to save fuel.

On May 18th, all the cows and calves were turned out to grass, and that made life a lot easier. I had to go to the fields to fetch them in for milking early in a morning and take them out again before going to school. Then it was the same again after school, along with anything else that needed doing. After the first week in June, the cows were taken out of the meadows and grazed in the pastures. The meadows were now chain harrowed, rolled and left to grow for hay, to be mown around the end of July or beginning of August, depending on the weather. This system gave the flowers and herbs chance to grow and seed, and was responsible for the beautiful flower-rich meadows of those days.

To the North of Wormhill

Looking towards the Plateau and Millers Dale from below Hassop Farm, Wormhill.

Haymaking at Hollinsclough. Above Harry Wheeldon, and below, the Slack sisters.

Cobwebs, hayseed and dust

The first time we got the hay at Wormhill was different from the Burrs. With over forty acres to harvest, Dad had hired casual labour so I was needed to load. We started on the big meadow, eight acres, and with not having a hay loader, there was a lot of hard work in the carting of it.

As soon as Dad got the chance, he hired an Irish labourer for the season. These Irishmen were usually small farmers themselves, and they were used to and willing to do hard work. Dad, knowing they only came over to this country to make money to subsidise the meagre living they made out of their own farms, treated them as equals, always giving them a room in the house instead of having to sleep in the barn or in a loft, as many other farmers had them do. They always ate with us and had the same food if they liked it, or Ma made them something else if they did not.

One job Hughie Caffee did when no hay was ready was to build up a gap which had appeared in a high wall. Towards evening Dad went to look how Hughie was getting on. When he got to where the gap had been, Hughie was just finishing off the setting of the top stones but to my Dad's surprise, the new piece of wall was only three foot high but four foot wide. When Dad explained to him that it should be higher than the width, Hughie replied, *"Ar for sure sir, should ever a wind strong enough blow it over, it would be one foot higher."*

The worst job in haymaking was filling in the last room in the lofts after the first filling had got hot and settled. It took at least three of you to get the hay back from the picking hole and back up onto the top of the mound. It was so hot that it was almost unbearable. The heat became trapped under the roof. My job was to press and stack the hay, starting right at the back and working forward. I was bent double, getting my hair covered in cobwebs, hayseeds and dust. It was good to get out into the fresh air again.

While I worked up in the loft, I always listened for the man unloading on the wagon, listening for his pitchfork to strike the boards on the bottom of the wagon. Then I knew then there was not much more left of that load to do, and I would soon be out into the fresh air with a cool drink. Farmers used to get barrels of what was called harvest beer for the older workers. There was always plenty to go at on most farms.

Another hard job was hacking, that is, after the mowing machine had cut the field, it always left some standing grass around the wall sides with large unmown corners. This was cut with a scythe, then collected with a fork and shaken out further into the field, so the haymaking machine could get at it. Every field was done like this until labour became scarce and then we used 'ivory scythes' - cows' teeth - as soon as the hay was clear; we turned the cows in to eat the grass from the wall sides .

Some time later Dad procured a big Morris car for which he got a Hackney licence. With no other taxis for five miles and only two buses a week, one on Saturday morning, the Morris was useful but not as fast as the old Vauxhall 14 had been. This was taken to pieces, and with the axles and chassis removed, and an extra axle, it made a six wheeled tow dray, bigger than anything else around. Because it was able to bring home much larger loads of hay and straw, it was highly prized. The only trouble was that it needed a lot of unloading!

Loading was a lot easier because we had acquired a hay loader. We only had to put the hay in windrows with the swathe turner, then hook the hay loader on behind the trailer and go along the rows of dry hay and the loader would pick up the hay and with a conveyor action, carry it up onto the trailer for two of us to move along and load it. It was loaded in the same way as hand loading but lifted mechanically. It cut out the need for a lot of labour, of which, in wartime, there was less and less.

When Dad bought it, it was not working. The two big drive wheels were seized up so much it took him a long time to free them and get them off. Then Dad turned the centres out by hand, using baring scrapers. Now he cut lubricating grooves in the cast centres, and drilled and tapped a hole into which he screwed a grease nipple. It gave no trouble after that. It was a Massey general-purpose loader and picked up grass, hay or sheaves - where the conventional hay loaders would only pick up dry hay. If you had one of those and it was a wet season and you had to make silage, you either lifted it by hand - a terrible job - or got a green crop loader as well. Yes, we had many years of good work out of that hay loader.

Then we got a pick-up baler which really revolutionised the hay harvest, making it easier to load and easier to stack on the wagons. It carried more weight and got a lot more into the lofts and barns and made it easier to feed in the winter. There was no more mauling with a cutting knife to cut the stacked hay into loadable slabs.

The other haymaking machine was the tedder. This was the villain of the hayfield and only used in catchy weather when we had to try and get the hay dry quickly. You could either back-kick the hay, by making rows, which went the same way as the wheels, then with the tines going faster than the wheels they would just flirt the hay out behind it. But if you changed the gearing, the drum would go in the opposite way to the wheels, bringing the hay up the front and over the top of the drum, throwing it out behind for yards and knocking all the seed out at the same time. This method got hay drier faster than any other method but a lot of the feed value was lost with the seed and it took a lot of rowing up ready for the hay loader. Some of it was in the next field anyway especially if it was windy

After the hay was finished, we used to have a harvest supper and what a party that was! There was plenty of everything - food and drink in plenty. That was when the home-made wines were tested. Some of these were very strong and many a days work was lost after sampling those homemade brews. The big tables were laden with homemade bread, cake and pies. There were boiled hams, home-cured of course, chicken, roast beef, lamb and pork, ox tongue, salted cooked, dressed and pressed into mould, sausages, cooked and left to go cold, onions of different kinds - spring, pickled, sliced in vinegar - and all kinds of homemade pickles, chutneys and so on. Then it was all topped up with cream and sherry trifles. This was a challenge and a chance for the ladies of the farm to show that they were good at this job as well as working in the fields alongside the men.

Little did we know that 1939 would be the last of a peaceful era of plenty.

Towards Blackwell from Monksdale Road, Wormhill.

Monks Dale.

Where the four dales meet

It was towards the end of August and I was looking forward to starting my new school at Tideswell. With haymaking done, instead of going to help others who had not yet finished, I now explored my new surroundings. I had seen Cheedale from the bottom of the fields, which ran across the top of the deep valley of the River Wye while we were haymaking and it looked very inviting, although it was about three hundred feet below the meadows.

I finished all my jobs early and off down the dale I went, taking my sheath knife with me. I took the track down past the old gamekeeper's bungalow where Mr Warhurst lived, down to the narrow gate and stile on the boundary of Cheedale. Once over the stile, it was like a different world. Everything was wild and uncultivated, rough and rocky.

I continued down the track. I could hear a stream on my right but could not see it for the thick undergrowth of gorse, blackberries and all manner of plants. On the steep bank to my left were lots of young ash plants of all sizes up to ten or twelve feet high, obviously self-seeded as they were so close together.

I climbed up the rocky bank, weighing up the trees as I went, and selected one of a pair which were growing too close together. I took my knife from its sheath, which was hanging to my left side, and used it to dig around the root of the ash plant, to see if the base was curved to form a handle. It was not, so I cut the ash off close to the ground, then removed the offshoots, and cut it off near the top to leave me with a six-foot quarterstaff.

Pleased with my new support, I went down the track towards the plateau. Just as the track levelled off, I could hear a waterfall to my right. I found the stream a few yards from where I stood as it disappeared over a cliff, dropping about thirty feet. I had not seen a waterfall before and I spent some time just standing there watching it. I went across the stream and up the bank to look at what was over the wall at the top. I quietly, peeped over and to my surprise there were rabbits everywhere.

I watched their antics for a while before I retraced my steps across the stream to the track. Turning right now, I crossed to the edge of the plateau and witnessed for the first time the breathtaking view where the four valleys meet. On my right was the valley leading to Wormhill, next Flagg Dale, then the dale we called Meadow Wood, tall pine trees one side and steep limestone cliffs shining on the other, divided by the River Wye. Lastly, on my left, Chee Torr, past which the river flows, crossed by a substantial footbridge lower down.

The track that I had come down continued down to the bridge, gently down the side of the dale. Although an ancient path or track, it had been improved in 1936 to allow a horse and cart or sledge to pass to take the materials down to build the bridge. Across the bridge, and down stream a hundred yards, there is a sheepfold and washing place. This one had a natural fold of overhanging cliffs on one side, the river on the other and a rock face on the third, probably making it one of the best sheepwashes in the peak district.

I sat down on a bare rock to take in all I saw before me. I wondered what kind of bridge had been down there before that new one had been built. I supposed it was a wooden affair, probably washed away in a flood or rotted with time. But what had been there hundreds of years ago? Perhaps just a long tree trunk? - and I imagined whether Little John and Robin Hood had met there and fought with quarterstaffs just like the one I had cut for myself.

I had been told that all this area was once part of Sherwood Forest and there was some kind of footbridge there when the Vikings came up the Wye and made a settlement at what is now called Wormhill. And what was there when the Ancient Britons had their settlement on the opposite hill? It was well placed, because this was the path wild migrating animals would have taken, the only way they could go, because of the sheer cliffs on either side, for a mile or so. Either side of this crossing, food would have been plentiful for the hunters, and even today there is an abundance of hazel trees on the dale side facing north, and on the south side there are wild strawberries, blackberries, raspberries and many other good things to eat. Yes, with a little knowledge of history, you could sit there and see it all before you, if you used your imagination.

After daydreaming for some time, I glanced up at the sun, and realised it must be about four o'clock, so I jumped up and made my way back home to the modern world.

Using stone

When visitors come to these hills and dales, they say how lucky we are to be living in such beautiful surroundings; old stone houses, farm buildings and bridges, dry stone walls, country roads that twist and turn as if made of ribbon, and quaint little dew ponds where cattle drink.

Yes, we are lucky to be living here. But luck did not find the thousands of tons of stone, sand, gravel and clay to build these things of beauty. The hands of men, women and children built and made what we have, by their brains, sweat, blood and aching backs.

When we think about it, the logistics were brilliant, for the materials had to come from somewhere local, and that somewhere was out of the ground, where it had been laid down by God's almighty hand.

All went well until in the 18th and 19th centuries, the big land grab was under way by outsiders much cleverer than us country folk. They had all the commons enclosed for themselves, except small parcels of land in each parish from where building materials were to be got - no good enclosing hard work!

These were allocated to the councils in whichever parish they lay, and vested in the surveyors of highways. These men were appointed yearly without pay by the parish council who were the highway authority of the day. The surveyors had the job of organising and overseeing the manpower made available to them. In days gone by, each household had to supply a man for one or two weeks, with farmers finding a horse and cart with a waggoner for one week without pay. Any more than a week was at a fixed rate of pay per day.

Stone was got out of these quarries and broken up by casual labourers needing a few shillings. Old men sat at heaps of large stones breaking them down to the size needed for the job in hand. The local stone was not hard wearing, so in the early

20th century, the limestone was brought from the bigger quarries around Buxton. Limestone is better wearing, being harder and not crushing so easily under the iron tyred wheels of the carts and waggons. But when wet it was very slippery.

As soon as funds and materials were available, the main roads were tarmacadamed and the days of the dusty white roads were mainly finished except for very minor roads. Even these got coated in the late thirties or forties, leaving only private unadopted lanes as an example of how the roads used to be.

So now we no longer have loads of stone being tipped in the old quarries and at the side of the road ready to be broken down to size, where using a napping hammer, the old men would sit napping in all weathers under old sacks.

Gradually, the bigger quarries installed crushers, mainly for the chemical industry, but as production grew, chippings and tarmacadam also became available for the roads.

The parish council's land began to be used for other things. Some was loaned as storage depots for the highway chippings and salt, but was still being used by local parishioners for such things as cutting the herbage for stock feed or as staging posts in snow, with most of the pieces of land being at the side of a road and kept clean by snow ploughs. It is not a lot of trouble to clear a space for a waggon to back off the road to off-load into farm tractors, trailers or sleds, leaving it to the farmers to get the produce home, be it fuel or food for man or beast. Even the mail goes by this route. In a big blizzard we have to make use of everything we have got, for when communications are cut by ten feet snowdrifts, we, the country folk, are on our own, when we live off the main roads.

Things began to change at the end of the war when heavy-winged snow ploughs were fitted on the front of armoured cars at first and then on six by six heavy waggons as they were released by the war office for civilian use. I remember the first such plough coming up into Wormhill from Millers Dale, escorted by fifty or sixty German prisoners of war with shovels to clear what snow fell back into the road after the heavy plough had gone through. Although by the time it came, we, that is the whole village, had dug our own way down to Millers Dale.

With the vicar on the lead shovel we had hacked our way slowly yard by yard through drifts up to twelve feet high. On a big drift the lead team would divide and dig from either side, throwing blocks of snow out over eighteen inches square. Yes, we are still animals when the need arises; the strongest in

The 1947 snow near Longnor.

front, followed by the older and the weaker in the rear, all doing as important a part as the other. When a whole village gets to work as a team in time of need they can move mountains.

All the people working on the road got paid by the hour. It was up to the council lengthsman to keep check on all this activity. A lengthsman was a man employed by the District Council to keep the roads tidy and clear - all culverts cleared, weeds and grass cut, and all the other jobs that are needed to maintain the parish roads and paths in good order.

While I was on my way to school once I saw two 'old gentlemen' starting work on a mere or dew pond. They had already marked out the circle and were taking the turf off. I looked in on them day after day and the hole got deeper until they came to rock, which they managed to remove without any explosives. The mere was not a big one - it was fifteen feet in diameter and six feet deep.

After the digging was finished, a layer of lime was put down, then cart loads of good yellow clay were brought to which water was added. The clay was pummelled with a clay mow, a wooden tool with an egg-shaped head and a 5-6foot stail. After pummelling the clay into the right consistency, a six inch thick layer was laid, starting at the base. After the layer of clay, a large flat base stone was laid at the centre, then it was paved on the clay all the way up.

Water was taken from these ponds on out-lying farms for all washing and drinking purposes until the 1930s. We stopped using this water for drinking about 1936 or 1937 when we started carrying drinking water from Mr Grindey's at Chelmorton, starting with 2 cans and ending up with a 17 gallon churn once a week.

When Grandad moved from the Burrs to Shireoaks, the cattle were driven up to the stable fields, where they turned left along Caxterway lane, then left again up Coal Pit Lane down to the flat. Here they turned right onto a green lane past Calton farm onto the A6, then right down the old coach road to Blackwell Mill, using the old ford to cross the River Wye. They then turned left up to Great Rocks Dale which is now closed by Tunstead Quarries, up Monkey Brow, before turning right towards Doveholes. Here they followed the A6 for a hundred yards, crossed up and over Martin Side, and took the second right for Tunstead and Chapel Milton, going under the viaduct and right at the Wash 250 yards further on. Here they turned left to the Breck farmyard and then went straight along the lane through twelve gates to Shireoaks farm.

It was a fifteen mile walk and this was the last time the route was used because Tunstead Quarries blocked the way the very same year and another route had to be used via Orient Lodge.

The drovers took sandwiches and drink with them. Taking cattle is far different than rambling. For the first two or three miles the cattle want to turn back, going onto any opening they see. Open gates had to be closed by the front runners. If it was an opening without a gate, one runner would have to stay in the gap while the herd went by and then get to the front again. Meeting oncoming herds could be a big problem. If you could hold one herd in a side lane while the other passed, it was not too bad - if there were enough of you. If there were no handy side roads or passing places, you could let one lot into a field holding them near the gate, ready for going on to road again.

We do not know when or where some of these lanes and drovers' trails may be needed again. They started to close with the coming of modern transport and are still being closed today.

The tracks are as old as the villages themselves, but many have been closed by various means over the past fifty years. Is this right?

The Brindley Well, Wormhill.

Hassop Farm, Wormhill.

WHIPPLETREES.

Page in Catalogue		£ s. d.		£ s. d.		£ s. d.
53	No. 1,	1 0 0	No. 2,	1 7 6		
	„ 4,	1 5 0	„ 5,	1 19 0	No. 6,	1 14 0
	„ 7,	2 1 6	„ 8,	2 8 0		
	„ 10,	2 9 0			„ 12,	2 15 0
	„ 13,	2 4 0				

SADDLE HARROWS.

		£ s. d.		£ s. d.		£ s. d.
56	No. 1,	4 17 0	No. 2,	4 5 6	No. 3,	3 15 0
	„ 4,	4 10 0	„ 5,	5 3 6		
57	Wheel Land Press	... ...			...	2 5 0
57	Wood Potato Harrows	... ...			...	5 5 0
	Iron ditto.	... ...			...	5 10 0

ZIG-ZAG HARROWS.

		£ s. d.		£ s. d.		£ s. d.
58	No. 00,	4 0 0	No. 0,	4 10 0		
58	„ 1,	4 16 0	„ 2,	5 2 6		
59	„ 3,	5 7 6	„ 4,	5 17 6	„ 5,	6 2 6
59	„ 6,	7 15 0	„ 7,	8 0 0	„ 8,	8 10 0

WOOD HARROWS.

			£ s. d.
59	No. 1 Small	... ...	4 17 0
59	„ 2 Medium	... ...	5 6 0
59	„ 3 Large	... ...	6 0 0
59	„ 4 4 in set	... ...	6 13 0

DRAG HARROWS. NO HANDLES.

		£ s. d.		£ s. d.		£ s. d.
60	No. 00,	4 12 6	No. 0,	4 17 6	No. 1,	5 2 6
	„ 2,	6 7 6	„ 3,	7 5 0		

DRAG HARROWS. WITH HANDLES.

		£ s. d.		£ s. d.
60	No. 0,	6 18 0	No. 1,	5 7 0
60	„ 2,	6 12 6	„ 3,	7 10 0
60	Pair with 22 teeth, £5 15 0			
60	ditto		Strong, £7 10 0	
	Pair with 30 teeth, £8 10 0			

HORSE HOES.

Page in Catalogue.					£ s. d.
62	Horse Hoe, No. 1	...	...	...	5 0 0
62	do. No. 2	...	...	...	4 10 0
63	do. No. 3	...	...	...	5 0 0
63	do. No. 3, 5 tine	...	...	...	4 10 0
63	do. No. 4	...	...	...	5 5 0
64	do. No. 5	...	...	...	5 5 0
65	do. No. 6	...	...	...	4 5 0
66	Steerage Hoe for Sugar Beet	...		...	11 10 0
67	No. 6 „ „ roots	...	...		9 0 0
67	No. 7 „ „ „	...	...		9 17 6
67	No. 8 „ „ „	...	...		10 12 6
67	No. 9 „ „ „	...	...		12 0 0
68	No. 3 „ „ corn and roots		...		8 10 0
68	No. 4 „ „ „	...	...		9 10 0
68	No. 5 „ „ „	...	...		10 10 0
69	Invincible Hoe for corn	...	...		4 15 0
69	„ „ roots	...	...		4 15 0
69	„ „ corn and root	...			6 15 0

FLAT ROLLERS.

70	20in., £15 15 0	24in., £17 15 0	26in., £18 15 0
	If with 2 cylinders 25/- less.		

SECTIONAL ROLLERS.

70	15in., £14 0 0	16in., £14 15 0

CAMBRIDGE ROLLERS.

71	16in., £16 0 0	18in., £17 10 0	20in., £18
	22in., £19 10 0	24in., £22 6 0	
	26in., £24 15 0	28in., £30 0 0	
71	2 Wheel Land Press	... ...	£18/10/0
3	ditto.	... ...	£21/10/0
	Driver's seat for all Rollers 20/- extra.		

ANGLE IRON AND WOOD BEAM PLOUGHS.

Page in Catalogue	Mark	No Wheels £ s. d.	One Wheel £ s. d.	Two Wheels £ s. d.	Steel Breast	Skim Coulter
5	XLSS Wood	6 15 0	[8 8]	6 Included	10/6	
6	XLSS Iron	8 8 6	10 2 6	do.	10/6	
6	Ditto (Long with all match appliances)	... ...	11 9 0	do.		
3	Ditto (Short ditto)	...	11 2 0	do.		
6	Ditto (Long & Short ditto)	...	12 7 6	do.		
6	Plough Sledge, SF	...	... ...	...	1 6 0	
6	Ditto. DF	...	... ...	...	1 11 0	

WOOD PLOUGHS.

Page in Catalogue	Mark	No Wheels £ s. d.	Two Wheels £ s. d.	Steel Breast	Skim Coulter
7	A	... 4 18 0	NAKED ... 8 0 0	... 4/6	... 10/6
7	CV	... 4 15 0	NAKED ... 7 15 0	... 4/6	... 10/6
8	L	... 4 9 0	NAKED ... 7 7 0	... 4/6	... 10/6
8	B	... 4 0 0	NAKED ... 6 10 0	... 4/6	... 10/6
9	LY	... 4 8 6	NAKED ... 7 0 0	... 4/6	... 10/6

IRON PLOUGHS.

Page in Catalogue.	Mark	No. Wheels	One Wheel	Two Wheels	Steel Breast	Skim Coulter
10	Lot 2	...	4 1 6	4 11 6	4/-	10/6
11	LNO	... 4 7 6	5 0 0	5 13 6	4/-	10/6
12	LN	... 4 12 6	5 5 0	6 0 0	4/-	10/6
12	LN Strong	6 5 0		7 11 6	Included	10/6
12	XLRC	... 6 12 0		8 1 6	do.	10/6
13	RN2	... 6 12 0		8 0 0	do.	10/6
13	XLRH	... 6 12 0		8 1 6	do.	10/6
14	KL2	... 7 15 6		9 7 0	do.	10/6
14	KL1	... 8 7 0		10 2 0	do.	10/6
15	CUM	... 7 15 6		9 2 6	do.	10/6
16	XLRLN	...		9 15 0	Included	10/6
16	XLRLS	...		9 5 0	do.	10/6
17	Subsoiler £2 5 0					
17	Sower, for Beans &c. £4 6 0					

DIGGER PLOUGHS.

Page in Catalogue	Mark	One Wheel £ s. d.	Two Wheels £ s. d.	Steel Breast	Skim Coulters
18	RUS 1 Strong...		8 12 6	Included	Included
18	RUS 1	... 7 4 0	7 15 0	do.	10/6
19	RUS 40	...	9 9 0	do.	Included
19	XLUR	...	10 14 0	do.	do.
20	FCL ...	...	8 16 0		do.
20	CHL ...	...	8 0 0		do.
20	No. 20	...	7 12 0		do.
21	CLP ...	...	9 9 0		do.
21	No. 30	...	8 0 0		do.
22	RUS WOOD	...	8 0 0	Included	do.
23	CWP	...	8 0 0		do.
23	CRP ...	...	9 2 6		do.
24	AD ...	...	5 5 0	Included	10/6
24	RN 1	... 5 8 0	6 0 0	do.	10/6
24	RN 1 Strong ...		6 5 0	do.	10/6
25	Snap Chain Lever 21/- extra.				
25	Improved Lever to land wheel 39/- extra.				

DIGGER PLOUGHS.

Page in Catalogue.	Mark	Two Wheels	Skim Coulter
26	DIG ...	... ... 9 9 0	... 12/-
26	GAL 1	... ... 8 11 0	... 12/-
26	DIG 2	... ... 10 2 6	... 12/-
26	DIG Deep	... ... 15 17 6	... 12/-

STEEL BAR POINT PLOUGHS.

27	LCS ...	... ... 8 0 0	... Included
27	CLS ...	... ... 8 15 0	... do.
27	CLS Strong ...	... 9 12 6	... do
27	CPLC ...	... ... 5 8 0	... 10/6

BEET LIFTERS.

28	Beet Lifter, Iron	... 5 0 0	
28	do. Strong	... 6 10 0	
29	do. No. 3	3 18 6	
	10in. Skeith and Clasp 15/- extra		
	Moling Attachment 10/-.		
	Subsoiling Shares 3/-.		
	Body for Beet Lifter £2.		

Ploughing and sowing

Dad had asked Mrs Bagshawe if he could plough the small meadow at Birk's Barn as it was very poor and sour. As a tenant, you used to ask the landowner's permission in those days. She thought about it and then agreed. So, late in August, after the hay was carted, Dad decided to start ploughing.

He set off with Bess in the cart shafts with the plough, swingle trees, plough harness, and anything else he might need, all loaded in the cart, with a new horse tied behind. Dad had only been gone half an hour when Uncle Jim arrived in the yard. He asked where my Dad was, so I told him he had gone to start ploughing. He said he would follow him to see what sort of a mess he was making. *"Come on with thee, Claude, jump in side-cheer."*

As soon as I was in, he was off. His Norton 600 cc 1927 model sounded perfect and we roared down Wormhill, past the post office, down the cutting and across the flat towards Knotlow. At the end of the flat, we turned left into the stack yard and then up the big pasture to where Dad had just finished marking out the little meadow, ready to start the first furrow. Seeing Jim, he said *"You timed that just right, our Jim,"* and handed Jim the reins. He walked over to the cart, sat down, lit a cigarette and let Jim get on with the ploughing. Jim was the professional at this game in our family.

After a short rest, Dad and I started to rebuild a wall gap that had fallen. Dad built the outsides while I filled the middle with small stones, passing any large ones over from my side of the wall when he needed them.

By the time we were ready to go home for tea and do the evening milking, Uncle Jim had ploughed about half an acre, not bad going for a pair of horses not used to furrow work. Uncle Jim was a professional ploughman, who worked hundreds of acres in his time. Before he had started, he had re-set our plough to suit the land to be ploughed so that it cut, turned and levelled the furrow like slicing through butter. It is far easier for both man and horses and makes a much better job when the tackle is set right.

During the following week, Dad finished the field off, letting me have a go at ploughing myself. When the field was finished we left it for the winter frost, snow and rain to do their work, breaking down the furrows and killing off most of the weed roots. We would be ready to start work in Spring to make a seed

bed for whatever we wanted to sow, by spike harrowing it several times over.
Is it possible to plough and sow,
but then to learn to march swinging your arms? No!

From the age of eleven, I slowly learned how to sow seed 'broadcast'. Before you can begin, you must first prepare the seedbed by making it as good as you have time to make it. Next, you need your bags of seed - oats or barley. We did not grow wheat because the season was too short at over 1,000 ft. above sea level. In addition to this, wheat straw has little feed value.

The bags were set out in a row the length of the field, about fifty yards apart and, where possible, thirty yards away from the longest wall and running parallel with it. While you were at the far end of the field, you would place a marker, ten feet from the perimeter walls. A marker would normally be a post or perhaps two stones placed on top of one another on top of the wall - anything as long as the marker could be viewed clearly from the opposite end of the field.

Now, going back to your starting point, you would need a seed-hopper. Then you adjusted the straps which went over the shoulders and around the neck. This made it easy to reach handfuls of seed. It was normally the job of one of the boys to carry the seed in a bucket to the man sowing the seed, which he would fetch from any of the bags placed in the field.

You were now ready to begin. You stood with your back to the end wall, about ten feet from the wall and looking down the field. The boy would tip his first bucket of seed into the hopper. With a right and throw and a left and throw, and so on, off you went, making straight towards the ten foot marker at the other end of the field, passing level with each bag, where the hopper was filled again with seed by the boy. Exact pacing was more important than speed - any areas which were missed would grow weed.

The proof of the sowing is in the growing. For a field neatly sown is easily mown.

There is a rhythm to sowing broadcast. Your arms and legs must be synchronised to work like a machine. Once you got the hang of it, you never lost it, just like riding a bike. Years later, whilst on military service, I had difficulty in trying to learn to march in step with my arms swinging correctly. Marching for miles was no trouble; the rough terrain was no trouble; but getting my arms to march in rhythm with my feet was hopeless, no matter how I tried. I could not get it right. After some time an understanding Major took me on one side and tried to put me right. Even he had to give up. If it had not been for my high artisan qualifications, I would have been in real trouble. Each time I got into a jam, thankfully, someone from Command workshop would ask for me to sort out a technical problem. So then it was goodbye to drill and marching for the time being.

It was not until I was home, helping with the spring work, and Dad asked me to sow some oats on the four-acre field, that it suddenly occurred to me where I was going wrong. The rhythm of marching was very much like, but opposite, to that of sowing. If you have mastered sowing by hand, it becomes almost impossible to march with arms swinging.

In September 1940, the field of oats needed cutting. One Sunday morning, two local characters came to ask for the job of cutting, tying and setting up the sheaves in stooks, or kivvers. A price was agreed and Dad found them a good scythe and stone each. Then they wanted a sub, so Dad gave them ten shillings each, and a gallon stone container of beer, and off they went down to the cornfield.

A day or two later, Mr Wilshaw, who had been on a walk around, came to Dad and said they hadn't cut much of the field. So off we went to have a look for ourselves. All they had cut were enough sheaves to make two seats where they had sat and drunk the beer, for the empty jar was lying on the ground nearby. We found out later they had drunk the beer and then gone to the Railway Hotel at Miller's Dale to spend their sub of ten shillings each. That was the end of that.

So we cut it ourselves with the reaping tackle on the mowing machine, collected it into sheaves and tied it by hand. We then set it up in kivvers to dry out and ripen, before carting and stacking it ready for winter feed.

To tie a sheaf, you collect a bundle about a foot across, then take a handful of straw stems, wrap them around the bundle, cross them over, twist until tight, then bend them under into a sheaf knot. To make a kivver, you pick up two sheaves and stand them up with the butts on the ground. Then you get two more and stand them up making four, then two more and then the same again.

It was in this field, the following year, that I found the first of many clues to what had gone on in the past. Whilst hoeing potatoes, I came across a flint. Now any flint that is found in this part of the country has clearly been carried here by man at some time in the distant past to make tools and weapons with. And when we first ploughed it, I could see three rings of darker soil about twelve to sixteen feet across, so it must have been a small stone-age village long, long ago.

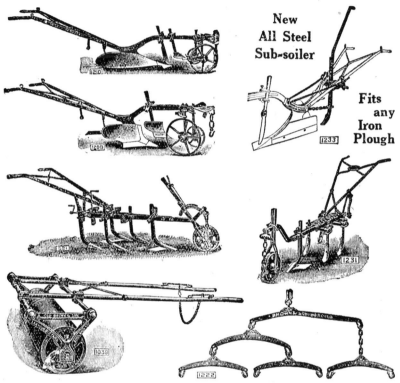

"You farmers will have to do as you're told"

In the Spring Mr Rowarth brought a Vauxhall 14 HP car to the Bagshawe Arms to try to sell to Dad. After a lot of bargaining, Dad paid Mr Rowarth £40 for it. It was three years old, and Dad said that was all it was worth. Its registration was BAL 913.

The first job it did was to take some strong lambs to Bakewell market. As we had no trailer, we took the back seats out of the car and started to load six lambs, but the first one in tried to escape through the opposite back door window, headbutting the glass and shattering it. So now we had to bolt a piece of plywood over the hole before we quickly loaded the lambs again, just getting them to market in time for the sale.

That car was used for many things, for example collecting and delivering fuel and oil for the tractors. The Fordsons used about one gallon of petrol a day for starting and running until the vaporising plate got hot enough for the TVO. You turned the two-way tap from petrol to TVO (kerosene USA). When you wanted to stop the engine while running on TVO you first switched the two-way tap off. To save fuel you had a small tin with a wire handle. You opened the drain cock on the carburettor bowl, hung the tin on the bowl, and caught the draining TVO. When the engine stopped the fuel was emptied back into the tank. To start again you closed the 'carb' drain cock again, turned the two way to petrol, pulled out the choke, and turned the starting handle sharply.

Yes, that car was used for many things but not for pleasure, petrol being

Rex at the Bagshawe Arms, guarding ENU 4, Dad's pride and joy.

tightly rationed. Night driving was very difficult because we just had slits of light showing through the blackout masks. It was even worse in fog, although fortunately the windscreen opened - it was cold and wet but you could see a bit better.

The only way we were allowed to use a car to get to Buxton was to collect farm equipment. I can remember on two occasions wanting to get to see the westerns *Jesse James* and *High Noon*. Ma rang Holme and Ash, ironmongers and agricultural engineers, for some plough shares to be left at the back of the gates in their yard. So we took the car loaded with as many people as it would hold, may be six of us, onto the parking area on Buxton market place. We walked across to the yard, picked up the plough shares from where they had been left at closing time - it now being about 7.30, and after locking the shares in the boot, we were free to go to the cinema.

Later on with haymaking approaching, Dad wanted a Bamlett mower. The only one he could find was one with a mounted petrol engine which drove the cutting-knife; a much better mower than the wheel drive - with these, when the horses stopped, the knife also stopped, so you had to back the horses and clear the cut grass from the cutter bar, before you set off again. With an engine-mounted mower, the knife never stopped.

It was bought off Sid Holland from Broken Cross, and I remember it being delivered; it was red and yellow with varnished shafts. It seemed a pity to get it dirty using it. But soon after unloading it was set to work. Now with a swathe turner, a tedder and a raking machine, we needed at least one more horse for carting the hay home. What with the roads being steep and one lot of fields three miles away, carting was going to be a big job. With one field mown, we were busy tedding and turning the new mown grass to make it into hay.

Uncle George and Aunt Bess, with their daughter Isabelle, arrived at the farm. She was a little younger than me. Bess and Isabelle stopped to help Ma and they put a basket of refreshments into Uncle George's old Morris 8 car to bring down to the hay field. He drove straight into the field. He was a character of the old school, a brilliant mechanic, and he was placed with the Royal Engineering Corps (REC) during the Great War.

As soon as he lifted the basket out, we all made tracks towards him. While we had a break Dad told George that we needed another horse for roadwork, and to Dad's surprise - because George did not like horses - he said they were dangerous at both ends - George said he would go and look for one.

Three hours later he was back with a broad grin on his face. *"Have you found one?"* Dad called. *"Yes, I have that,"* he replied. *"How big is it; is it quiet?"* *"It's big enough for what you want, but it'll kick if you're not careful. Anyhow it'll be here in an hour or so".*

Sure enough a wagon soon arrived in the yard. It was not a cattle wagon as we expected, but a flat wagon with an orange Fordson on it!

When Mrs Bagshaw heard of the tractor, the first in Wormhill, she came to look for herself.

Auntie Bess with Isabelle, Muriel, Joyce and Gwen.

Although there was one at Hargate Wall, Dad's was the first one on any of the Bagshaw estates. When she saw it, she said to Dad, *"That is the biggest white elephant that ever came into Wormhill,"* and marched off in disgust. But that tractor ploughed and cultivated hundreds and hundreds of acres in the years of need that followed, producing many tons of badly needed food!

On one occasion, Mr Beresford at Dale Head wanted a nine-acre stubble field ploughed and sown, before he took a short break. They were going away on the Saturday morning and he had asked us to plough and disc the field so that it could be sown before he went away. Now on the Wednesday before, it had not even been ploughed and he was getting upset with us. Anyhow, I arrived in the field early on Thursday morning and had set it out ready to plough. As he arrived, he was complaining: *"It's too bloody late now. We can't possibly get it sown before Saturday."*

"Don't worry," I said, *"I'll do the best I can. We've come to you as soon as we could. Even we can't be in two places at once."* With that he took out his watch and said something else, but I couldn't hear him.

I revved up the Fordson and struck off down the field, starting the first gathering. About two hours later, Alf was back after his milking. He had brought my breakfast, a basket with hot bacon sandwiches and a can of tea. When I met him on the headland at the top of the field, I stopped for the first time, and shut down the revs but I did not stop the engine as it would be too hot

to start again. I took the basket off him. He said, *"By gum, yow are moving."* I nodded, put the basket safe on the back axle and I was off again, eating and drinking as I went. In just eight hours that nine acres was ploughed, and by the end of the next day it was disced, harrowed, sown and rolled. Mr Beresford was so pleased, he gave me not only food and drink, but two pounds for myself as well, the equivalent in today's money of thirty pounds.

When the disc harrows came, Dad had them unloaded in Birks Barn pasture, near to where they were needed first. As soon as it was dry enough he disced the plough field four times to make a good seed bed, then sowed oats broadcast, a job at which I became very skilled when I was older. Next he spike harrowed it lightly and, to finish the task, he rolled it.

This job had only been done about a week when a pompous gentleman arrived in the yard with a handful of maps. *"Mr Fearns?"* he asked. *"Yes,"* replied Dad. *"Good,"* he continued, *"I'm from the War Ag. I have come to inform you that you will have to plough and grow oats or barley on at least two acres of your farm."* With Dad not showing a lot of enthusiasm for the job, the man turned a bit nasty, *"You do know FEARNS, there's a war on and you farmers will have to do as you're told?"*

That did it. Dad stood up to him and retorted, *"Firstly, I've got a proper name and if you call me FEARNS again, you will need help to get you back to where you came from. Secondly, while you over-educated *****s have been sleeping, I've been ploughing. In fact, more than my share is already ploughed, sown and growing. If it was left to such as you, the country would starve. I can see by your hands you have never done a day's hard work in your life. Now get out of this yard and don't let me set eyes on you again".* With a lot of gasping and whimpering the Ministry man returned to his car and left.

This 'gentleman' had already been to other farms lower down the village, upsetting most with his tactless, domineering attitude. Two of the farmers, knowing how Dad dealt with drunks and yobs who started to throw their weight about at the inn, had come, unbeknown to Dad, to observe from a distance. I don't think they were disappointed.

Two days later, two different kind of men turned up to see Dad, saying that they had come to discuss the land which was about to be ploughed. They apologised for the first caller. Dad did not accept their apology, but said, *"What land?"* *"Well that is what we want to discuss with you. We have seen the job you have made of field No 1 and congratulate you on it. What we want to know is why you chose or selected that one and what your future programme is with regards to this particular field?"*

"This is not for the benefit of that clown who came the other day is it?" Dad asked rather sternly.

"No," said one of them, *"It is not. I was his superior and I can assure you that he has departed under a very black cloud and will never have anything to do with agricultural management again. One of your good neighbours contacted me yesterday, and his story did not match the report my man had placed before me earlier. So I contacted other farmers he had visited, as a result of which I fired him. Thinking about it, his only qualifications were that he had been a manager in one of the colonies. Now can we let bygones be bygones and get on with the future?"* He held out his arm to shake hands with Dad.

He introduced his partner, saying he was the new man trying to tackle a big job and must have the farmers' support to do it, whereupon Dad shook hands with him too, one phase now behind him, ready to start afresh.

"Well," said Dad, *"I ploughed the field because it was not growing much*

of quality. One obvious reason for that is because it was a long way from the muckheap in the farmyard. Another is that it was only half ploughed and the last time was many years ago. Another reason is that the soil is very acid. I told all this to Mrs.Bagshaw when I asked her permission to plough. My own programme is this: I have sown oats this year to check the acidity in the soil; next year I plan to grow one half swedes and the other half potatoes, then the following year rotate, with swedes or cabbage where the potatoes were and potatoes on the other half. After that I intend to sow oats under-sown with a good grass mixture. Any questions?"

"Very good, very good indeed," the superintendent said, turning to his colleague and saying, *"It's in your corner now".*

"May I congratulate you, Mr Fearns, and ask a few questions?" Dad just nodded his head for it was the first time this man had spoken and Dad had not weighed him up yet. *"Did you have the soil tested? If not, how did you know it was acid? Will you have the time and labour to see the programme through and why under-sow instead of reseeding with grass alone?"*

Dad replied, *"As to number one, I did not have the soil tested. I knew it was very acid by the plants that were growing in that field. Some were doing well while others had a job to survive and some were not present at all. Secondly, we will have to make the time and use what labour we have, with the potatoes being the most labour intensive to harvest. Anyone who helps will get a share. I think food will be worth more than money by then. As for seeding down with grass only, you will only get a light crop if any, in the year of sowing, with the seasons being short and late at this altitude. But under-sown with oats, you do not lose a year's crop and it will give cover, promoting the growth of more frugal grasses and clovers"*

"Do you think all should be ploughed and later reseeded?"

"No," Dad said, *"Most yes, but all, no."*

"Why? And which should not?"

"There are two kinds that spring to mind. The first are steep fields close to the rock where erosion may set in and the second, most important, are some of the old meadows rich in herbs and flowers. If they were ploughed, it would be not only foolish but criminal to plough, for they could never be replaced and the country would be poorer for it".

They asked Dad what implements he had for the tractor. They could see some of these in the open shed at the bottom of the yard, including disc harrows. Dad explained that he was also building a heavy trailer which would do general work and would carry muck, hay and straw - *"you name it,"* he said.

"Would you be prepared to do ploughing under contract for other farmers? It will mean you may have to employ someone yourself. But for harvesting, there will soon be land girls available".

Dad told them to let him know the price he could charge for work done on contract and where it would take place, so that he could then make his mind up.

With that they said good-bye.

Dad at Wormhill.

Dad, Muriel and Me.

The footbridge at Cheedale.

A white wilderness

After the corn harvest came the potatoes. We usually got a lot of help at weekends on this job from the people who wanted some for the winter. After that, we lifted the swedes, and the autumn ploughing got into full swing. Those tractors were never still. Even when the snow came, they would be out for the council, snow ploughing.

The snowploughs were nothing like those of today. They had been horse-drawn years before and were just made out of heavy planks of timber, but if the snow was fresh and had not been trampled by other vehicles, the old snow plough made a good job. The local roadman had to go with you and with the tractors in those days. Having no cabs, it was very cold for them. They were very often glad when we came to a drift and the tractor could not get through. They could start digging by hand to get warm again.

The first move early in the morning was down to Miller's Dale, if we could get. That would depend on how much snow had fallen in the night. Another factor was the wind, as it did not need a lot of snow to fall if there was a wind, to blow it off the fields into drifts. If the wind was coming from the South East, we could expect there to be a big drift on the flat just below Chapelsteads, where the wind swept all the snow out of the big meadow and through the gateway to pile up against the high wall on the opposite side of the road. It did not take long to fill the whole road to a depth of five to seven feet. It would be the same at all the other gateways along the flat - yet the radio might announce that two inches of snow fell in the Peak District overnight, giving false impressions to travellers not knowing the area.

If the wind was coming from the North, the whole road would be full up to the top of the walls, for the North road wall is a retaining wall, with the fields being higher than the road. The wall was two feet on the field side and four or five on the roadside, so that the wind swept the snow off the field to the North and filled the road full from wall top to wall top. That meant a lot of digging.

Sometimes the blocked road was abandoned altogether, and a track was made across the field, pulling a gap through each wall, where there was no gateway, for the horses, who would pull sledges with churns of milk tied on them to get them to the railway station. On a long snow this was the only link with the outside world, with the returning sledges bringing any empty churns and food, mainly bread, back to the village.

If snow began to fall during the day and children were at school, a close eye was kept on the weather. If only a few flakes were falling and the sky did not look too bad, the children from the outlying farms were sent home on their own. But if it started to snow heavily, and it looked bad, the teachers would try to make sure that someone would come for them. If it took them an hour or more to walk home in normal weather, it would take longer in snow and within half an hour what had been green fields could become a white wilderness, and very dangerous.

One Friday morning, after the milking was done and the cattle in the yard cleaned out and fed, the churns of milk were rolled out to the milk stand ready for the wagon to pick them up. It called to collect milk at each farm on its way through the village, starting at Chapelsteads and finishing at Wormhill Meadow. Now, with a full load, it carried on to Manchester.

While these jobs were being done, I went to feed the young cattle kept at the buildings at the back of the school. It was a funny morning: there was no wind, a lot of low cloud and it was warm. For the last week, a flock of fieldfares had been hovering around the village, which was not a good weather sign - and Miss Davies, the headmistress, had put a rug over the radiator of her car, parked on the side of the road outside the school gates, although there was no need as there was no frost about.

After letting the cattle out for water, I cleaned them out and placed hay in their cratches as a bribe to get them inside again so I could tie them up. Sometimes they would rather play and they led me a right dance before I could get them in, especially as the winter got older and the smell of spring stronger. With it being a warm morning, I expected trouble from them, but when I opened the shippon door, they were all waiting to come in - in fact, they tried to get in two at a time.

Anyhow, I tied them up and set off down home. Something was different now. It had suddenly gone colder with an East wind picking up. I knew now why the cattle were in a hurry to get inside - there was some really bad weather coming and it would not be long.

I rushed home and went to feed and water the stock at what we called the back of the Hall - we usually went on the footpath through the churchyard. These cattle did not even want to go out so they had to have some nut stick persuasion to go to the mere to drink. As soon as they had drunk, they were back waiting to get inside.

It had only taken me ten minutes to feed, water and clean out whereas it usually took thirty minutes. The wind had got stronger now, the evergreen trees and shrubs in the churchyard were twisting and bending with the wind, and as I passed through the kissing gate into the next farm before home, there was snow in the wind.

I met Mr Harold Mosley as I crossed his yard. *"What do you think it is going to do, Claude?"* he said looking up at the sky. *"We're in for some snow, no doubt about that,"* I replied, wanting to move on, to get everything else done that needed doing before the storm struck. *"I suppose we should be getting the young stock off the Middle Hills down towards some shelter. I better send Stanley and someone else for them,"* Mr Mosley said. *"I'll give them a hand, even if only from Peak Forest road end."* I offered. *"They'll take some driving down the village with all its bolt holes."* *"That's very good of you, Claude,"* he started to say, but I was gone.

Mr Mosley told Stan to get the yard jobs done as quickly as possible, then take some one with him to Middle Hills and collect all the stock and bring them back. Meanwhile he said he would organise getting a shed ready for them. At 11.30am they had set off expecting to be back in about 3 hours with the cattle.

The headmistress of the school, sent the outlying children home at 11.00am. With no communication with the outlying farms in those days, everyone had to rely on instinct as to what the weather was going to do, from the parents to the schoolteachers. The school closed at twelve midday, and the local children were soon home, with those going to Tunstead, the next village, going in a group. But the children from Wormhill Meadow, who were usually brought to and fro by car, waited at the school for the transport to turn up and it didn't come. The storm got worse and no one in the village knew about the children now stranded outside the locked school.

The storm had now turned to a blizzard. The village is always sheltered, with all its trees, and being lower than the surrounding land, so the four children set off walking up Wormhill in the direction of their transport. But their transport was fast in deep snow, in a lane miles away. The farmer-driver had seen the change in the weather coming and had set off at 11.00 am for the school, before the storm struck. He had also misread the weather, for the group of four farms which are called Wormhill Meadow are also comparatively sheltered, in contrast with the lanes and road between there and Wormhill. He had only gone half a mile when he got hopelessly stuck in drifts up to five foot deep, but he managed to get out of the car and walk back to the farm to get help.

The plan now was to walk along the footpath to Wormhill, the nearest route being about one mile. But it would be necessary to cross Flagg Dale en route, which was a dangerous place in good weather, never mind now. At 1.00pm, two of the fittest farmers set off for Wormhill School, reaching Wormhill at two, only to find the school empty and locked. What thoughts went through their minds? Where were the kids? Where had they gone? Had they gone to Tunstead with the others or had they set off walking the nearest way home and got caught in the blizzard and got lost? Where were they? And it would be dark early, and then what?

While this drama was unfolding, Mr Wilshaw, the council lengthsman, came into the yard and asked Dad to take the snow plough to Millers Dale. Dad went to get his coat and I started the Fordson, drove it out into the yard to where the snow plough was parked, backed up to it, then hooked on the heavy chains used to tow the old fashioned machine. Dad was togged up in a heavy coat and a good pair of gloves and checked everything was ready.

Tractor, plough, three men and three spades, Dad drove off for Millers Dale, with Mr Willshaw and I walking behind to keep warm. We went well until we got to the flat beyond Chapel Steads; the wind was blowing the snow off the fields and piling it up against the walls, filling the road with snow. But the blown snow was very powdery, so the Fordson, with heavy skid chains on, kept going through. In these situations you gave it its head and full power (we are still horse men at heart). When we got past Birk's Barn, we were in the shelter of Knotlow, so there was far less snow in the road, and getting to the station yard was no trouble, and here we turned round to head back.

Mr Willshaw rode on the tractor up to Wormhill, and we carried on up the village with little snow under the shelter of the trees; but reaching Hill Green

Lane End we were back in the blizzard again. We carried on to the crossroads where Wormhill, Tideswell, Hargate Wall and the road for Peak Dale meet. At this point Dad turned the tractor round to go home; it was about 2 pm. I took my spade now and went looking for the cattle. I carried on along past Hargate Hall looking to see if the big iron gates to the Hall were closed.

I made good progress along the sheltered road, but as I neared the point where the lane to Hargate Wall comes out onto the main road the blizzard hit me again, and it was slow progress to the Peak Forest turning. Here I put my back to the wind and waited, stamping my feet now and again to keep warm. After about 10 minutes, I heard them coming, and after a few more minutes I saw them looming out of the snowy mist. I started to call them and when they were close enough, I walked out in front of them, talking to them all the time, getting them to follow me. I turned into Hargate Wall Lane End, now driving the cattle past me along the road for Wormhill.

Now Stan had not seen me, and, not knowing I was there, he got over the wall into the field between the two lane ends, and with the snow being blown off the middle of the field he could run across it and over the wall into the Hargate Wall Lane to stop the cattle bolting down it looking for shelter. When he saw me there in the lane he shouted something. I shouted back, *"What?"* and listened hard, and removed the scarf from round my ears. I could hear something strange, like a whimpering from under the snow. It seemed to be coming from under the wall. I yelled for Stan to come. Then we both listened. Then we started to dig like mad with our hands - and we found these children huddled under the snow. We knew nothing of them being lost and the drama that was unfolding in the village.

The children had made their way slowly to the top of Wormhill, turned left along past Hargate Hall, still in the shelter of the thick woodland either side of the road but then the wind and snow had hit them hard. They had managed another 100 yards as far as Hargate Wall Lane End, before they had hidden by the wall for shelter - where we found them.

We could have carried the two younger ones, but we realised we had to try to get the children warm and the only way to do that was to make them walk. They were not very keen but were soon back in the shelter of the trees and, as we followed the path the cattle had made, they soon got some warmth back into their little bodies.

As they trudged the mile back into the village, they were now following the cattle. The animals now realised they were going home and they followed the lead cow right back into their own farmyard, which was as well, because by now it was black dark.

All were now safe in shelter of one kind or another. As in so many other times of need or emergency the taproom at the Bagshawe Arms was open with a good log fire; always a welcome to traveller or local in need of shelter. Once we got the children in side Ma organised some dry clothes, probably belonging to my sisters.

By now the two farmers from Wormhill Meadow had heard where the children were and had come and found them. After some hot warming food, it was time for them to get home and plans were made. It was a frosty moonlit night so travel would be good so we lent them a sledge on which the small children could ride if necessary. Two young men from the village escorted the party as far as Flagg Dale, and they watched them make their way safely across to the flatter fields on the other side. Soon they were all safely home.

The 1947 snow at Chelmorton.

That should square things a bit

In those early days, an old gentleman used to come to the Bagshawe Arms, after collecting his pension, with a pony and a small cart or tub. He used to drive in through the gate to the inn yard, tie the pony to the back of the open gate, so as to keep it well clear of the drive, then go in for a pint or two.

One hot day early in June, he tied up his pony as usual, but with it being such a hot day, he had more to drink than normal. We watched him as he staggered out, untied the pony - it seemed he had a special knot and all he had to do was to pull the loose end, then throw it over the pony's neck - and he fell into the cart and went to sleep. The pony took him home.

The next time he really got a skinful, we watched him closely into the inn. Now we untied the pony, took it out of the shafts pushed the shafts between the gate bars at the right height, then put the pony back into the shafts on the other side of the gate, tying the halter in a similar knot, but tied to nothing. The old man came out of the inn, went to the pony's head, pulled the halter rope, threw it over the pony's neck. He staggered to the back, fell into the cart and said *"go on"* before falling sound asleep. The pony could go nowhere, so there it stood.

About three hours later - just as we were finishing milking - the old man roused himself and looked around expecting to be at home. He got hold of the reins and said *"go on"* to the pony. The gate was a strong one and fastened at both ends, so the pony could not go. The old man got out to see what was the matter, and seeing the gate between the pony and cart, he swore at it *"How the hell have you got in this mess?"* and stood there scratching his head.

Luckily, a lad was carrying buckets of milk from Glebe Farm to Knotlow Farm on a footpath which crosses the Bagshawe Arms Yard, Knotlow Yard and onto the Church. He helped the drunken old man to sort out the situation, pulling the shafts out of the gate and re-shafting the pony.

Another character was Mr Dick Taylor. He looked like someone out of the wild west of America, with tough leathery features, finished off with a neatly cultivated moustache. He was a craftsman of the hills, able to work wonders with anything that was at hand, be it stone, wood or metal. He made and erected his own father's gravestone. Stone is the wrong word for it as it was made out of black bog oak and stands in St Margaret's churchyard to this day.

His favourite pastime was making wines and collecting plants, roots, flowers and berries for the job. As the seasons passed, he had found, with trial and error, a way of making them super strong. Some wines he brewed and bottled, then as haystacks were being built, he would place the bottles in amongst the hay. When a lot of hay is put together, after about three days, it gets very hot. Normally the bottles would explode under such heat, but with the great pressure of the hay all around them they never did. Months later when the cooled hay was removed to feed the cattle in the winter, Dick was there to collect his prized bottles.

Every Sunday lunch-time he would be sitting at the Bagshawe Arms on a chair on the right hand side of the fireplace in the tap room, from where he could keep an eye open for the ramblers coming up the road from Miller's Dale, either off the bus or from the railway station. By the time they had walked the mile or so up to Wormhill they were usually ready for a drink.

When he saw a likely candidate coming, he would get off his chair and move to the middle of the room to see if they turned into the gateway for the inn. If they did, he would put his plan into motion. No matter how much beer he had in his pint pot, he would quickly drink it down to leave an inch or so in the bottom.

When the ramblers had settled down with their drinks, he would bid them good day and start telling his yarns, sipping at the last drop of beer as he did. If no one offered to buy him another pint, he would wait till he got to a very interesting bit of his story, then pause, finish the last drop of beer and leave his yarn in midstream, knowing full well that someone would prompt him to carry on. He could usually get four or five pints this way.

Now he was neither hard up nor a scrounger, for as they left, which was usually at closing time, he would accompany them, knowing that they would be going past the house where he lived. On getting near to home, he would return the hospitality and invite them in for a drink of his special homemade wines.

Once they had accepted his hospitality, they never forgot it and came back many times, bringing unwary friends with them but never drinking quite as much home-made wine a second time themselves.

The first time we realised what he was doing was soon after we had taken the Bagshawe Arms. It was a nice Spring morning, a good morning for ramblers to be about. Dick was having his usual Sunday morning drink but his interest was on the road. Sure enough, he was rewarded when six ramblers came up the road and into the yard. He was soon putting his act on for them.

Dad was in the tap room and immediately thought he was scrounging,. Fortunately one of the other regular customers saw, and got Dad to go outside with him on some pretence. Once outside, the old man asked Dad what he made of Dick's performance. *"I think he is an old scrounger and I am going to stop him"*. *"No, you're wrong there, lad,"* the old man replied, *"You musna interfere. One of those ramblers has enjoyed Dick's company before and he has brought his unsuspecting friends for the same treatment. Old Dick will bring you more customers this summer than anyone else."* So Dad decided to watch and learn.

Later on, as normal, Dick went off up Wormhill with them. The next time we saw him was about three hours later. We had just started milking when Dad spotted Dick coming slowly down the road. Now, from the shippon, you could only see the top half of passers by because the wall hid the bottom half, but apparently Dick was using his stick to drive or goad something along the road. Dad said, *"The sheep must have got out and Dick's bringing them home"*.

But when he got to the gateway, we could see it was not sheep, but six ramblers creeping on hands and knees. If they tried to stand up they fell down but they could just about manage to creep. Somehow we managed to get them into the empty loose box and with some good clean straw, bedded them down for the night. Next morning they were as right as rain. Ma gave them a good breakfast and Dad took them down to Miller's Dale to catch a train back home.

The walker that had been before must have thought that Dick had forgotten him. Dick did remember and decided he was going to have a good laugh at his friend's expense. So he had given them some of his old strong wine, taking an equal amount himself. Dick was used to it, and the one that had been before was only going to have one glass and let his friends have as much as they wanted. But in the event they all only needed one each to knock them down.

They came back to the Bagshawe Arms often after that but did not go for any more of Dick's wine, even though they were the best of friends.

In the Tap Room the fireplace was one of the old traditional farm types with a big oven on the left, a fire in the middle and a boiler on the right. The boiler held about six gallons of water and had a lid about a foot square on the top for filling with buckets of cold water and getting hot water out with a ladle. One night, towards the end of November, I was sitting in the Tap Room watching Dick and Mr Wilshaw playing dominoes against two other locals. I had gone in there out of the way because Dad was sorting out some business in the living room with someone.

There was a good log fire burning in the grate and in the oven Ma was cooking a big cock chicken ready for a small party that had booked a meal for the next day. Each time she came in to serve drinks, she looked in the oven monitoring the progress of the chicken roast - but she was not the only one keeping an eye on it. When he judged it right, old Dick knocked his pot on the Tap Room table to let Ma know the group wanted filling up and, unusual for him, asked for a packet of crisps. He asked how much they were, then, after an argy-bargy as to whether they should be free with the beer, he grudgingly paid the tuppence on top of the beer money.

As soon as he got the crisps, he took out the small wrap of blue paper containing the salt and popped it into his waistcoat pocket. Ma's back was turned to put the money in the drawer we used as a till, and, just as she was going back in to the living room, he called to her. *"Eh up missis, there is no salt in this bag o'crisps."* Ma continued into the kitchen, grabbed a salt pot and brought it back for him. Turning to me, she scowled, *"Are you stupid, why didn't you get it for him?"* and marched off along the passage into the house.

As soon as she had gone, although they were in the middle of a game, Dick swept all the dominoes to one end of the table, got up, turned to the oven and opened the door. Taking off his cap, he used it to get hold of the roasting tin and pulled it out of the oven. He took a log out of the bucket standing by the boiler in his other hand, and used it to balance the roasting tin which held the now cooked chicken which he placed in the middle of the table. He wafted his cap to cool it down as quickly as possible, and in a few minutes they were able to set about their feast, using the salt Ma had unwittingly supplied.

Now I had learned not to interfere if you don't want to get involved, and I kept out of it. In a few minutes there was nothing left except the bones, so Dick quietly put the roasting tin, complete with bones, back into the oven and drank up. At this point, I thought they would get out of the way but no, he knocked for Ma to come and serve more beer!

The previous time she had come in, with all the kerfuffle about the crisps - which now lay uneaten on the table - she had forgotten to look at the chicken, but this time she remembered. Opening the oven door she saw immediately what had happened. I will not repeat what she said, particularly when she realised that she had even been foolish enough to supply the salt to go with the splendid meal. Turning on me she said, *"Why didn't you stop them?" "Well"* I said *"I'm STUPID, you said so yourself, not ten minutes ago."* With that she marched off in a huff! The problem now was what would Dad do about it. So they all listened hard and soon got the answer. Ma must indeed have told Dad but all we heard in the Tap Room was a roar of laughter from Dad. So his friend Dick could breathe a sigh of relief. *"We're o'rate,"* he said.

And that was that! Or so we thought. But about seven o'clock the next morning, we had got ready for milking when Dick turned up, carrying a large brown carrier bag. *"Here,"* he said to Dad, *"Put this in the oven before Missis gets up." "No,"* said Dad, *"You ate it. You put it in the oven yourself. Claude will go in with you and help you."*

We had to light the fire in a morning to boil the kettle to make a drink, so, by the time Dick and I took the chicken in, there was a good fire going. I opened the oven damper so the fire would draw under it and get it hot, and Dick put the carrier bag down on the ironing board that Ma had left out. It was a bit rickety and nearly collapsed under the weight, but we managed to get the chicken into a roasting tin and bunged the lot into the oven where we left it. *"There, that should square things a bit,"* said Dick as he went off home.

When Dick came the next Sunday morning, he brought Ma a present wrapped up in a long beet pulp bag. Spotting me, he said, *"Here, take this to your mother but take the bag off before you take it in the house".* I did as he bid. When I got to the back door, I called Ma and told her Dick had sent her a present. Opening the bag, we found he had made her a new ironing board of oak. It was and still is the best I have ever seen and, fifty years later, my sister still uses it.

Our family at Wormhill before the move.

Mum.

Dad and Auntie Win.

In case of invasion

As August came to an end, the whole village was buzzing with talk as to whether there would be a war or not. Then, early one Sunday morning in September, an announcement was

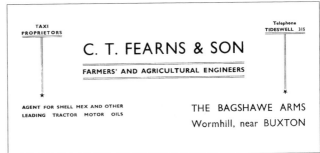

given out on the wireless that the Prime Minister, Mr Chamberlain, was going to speak to the nation. At the appointed time, everyone was indoors to listen to what he was going to say.

I was sitting on a strong chair near the doorway that led into the house when the announcement came through. Mr Chamberlain was talking in a shaky voice, and said that, in spite of his efforts for peace, a state of war now existed. A dull hush came over everyone and two minutes later the air-raid sirens wailed out. Fortunately it was only a trial run to let us know what they sounded like, and to test them. Actually in the Buxton area these were only the quarry sirens which had always been used, to warn of blasting, but now, until the end of the war, they were to sound in the event of enemy aircraft approaching. They had to use other means to warn of blasting. Later on, the church bells too were only to be rung in case of invasion.

During the following week, evacuees started to arrive in the village, mainly mothers with babies. The councillors had the job of finding them homes, one to each house in the village, or more, if we had the room. As usual, some would not have any at all. The Vicar, having a large vicarage, took in four or five families. The women and children were moved out of the cities because it was thought the Germans would send waves of bombers over as soon as war was declared, as they had done in Spain and other places. But the bombers did not come, so after a few weeks, the evacuees started to go home again.

A blackout was imposed, which caused a lot of problems on farms through the winter of 1939-1940, as they had to milk and feed cattle in the dark.

Now there came evacuees who were sent to Tideswell and these were different. They were sent as a complete school, pupils and teachers together, and this meant now that they had school in the mornings and we had it in the afternoon. So we only did half days, although later on they managed to fit us all in at once.

Needless to say, there were many fights as to which were the better fighters, town or country, but during air-raid practice we were all friends again. The drill was held when the sirens were sounded. All the pupils who lived in Tideswell would immediately go home, taking one or another with them to shelter from enemy activity, while the remainder of the school would run to take shelter in a three hundred yard trench which had been dug when the retaining wall was built along the roadside to the South West of the school.

These practices were no games for me. By now we knew what had happened to the people of Poland under aerial bombardment. After each exercise there was a roll call, after which Mr Armstrong the Headmaster would remind us that when the real air raids came, we might have only a few minutes to get to shelter and that, if we did not act quickly and properly, the roll call after it would be much shorter! We all knew what that meant.

School leaving age then was fourteen, although I did not go to school much after the war broke out. The school was overflowing with the extra population of evacuees, so one or two were not missed.

I did not want to do farmwork if I could help it, but I did not know what else I really wanted to do. Dad was very understanding and said I should get a trade. He saw the local joiner to see if he wanted a lad to work for him and then Joe Sellers, the blacksmith. But both of them said they did not have enough work to warrant another pair of hands.

The only other employment was the quarry. Now Dad in his wisdom always said that the farm tractors, which were powered then by petrol and TVO, would all be diesel in the near future. How right he was. The only places where there was a workshop to be found working with diesel engines were the bigger quarries. So as I neared 14, I went to Alcar House to see Mr Swarbrick, the personnel manager for I.C.I. He told me to come back when I was fourteen and he would see where and if he could fit me into the right job.

My full time farm days were numbered as Dad had got someone who wanted to learn farming and to work with animals - and I wanted to be an artisan.

Luck Money

During the first months of war, a few faces disappeared from the village. I remember that the families of Kirkham, Bramwell and Drury were among the first to lose members. Two of those young men never returned.

The war was going very badly. Most of Western Europe had fallen into enemy hands with the British Expeditionary Force having to escape through Dunkirk. The Local Defence Volunteers were hurriedly formed, consisting of anyone who had a weapon - from sidearm or .410 bores, to heavy hunting rifles - and could use them. Most of the country mobs were fully armed one way or another. One big advantage they had was that they knew the terrain, which made up for what they lacked in firepower.

The main aim, in case of invasion by airborne troops, was to take and hold the canisters of arms and ammunition when they landed. So fallen trees were dragged and left in the middle of all long, flat fields in which an aircraft or glider might land. All bridges near the South and East coasts were mined, ready to be blown up if need be. The sky was watched night and day for any signs of enemy activity, if the enemy was sighted the church bells would ring to call to arms.

The messenger corps was formed, with two boys of thirteen to sixteen to act as runners with messages, in case of communication breakdown. So there I was in public service! And have been ever since, one way or another, for fifty years!

Invasion did not come but the bombers did. A bomber's

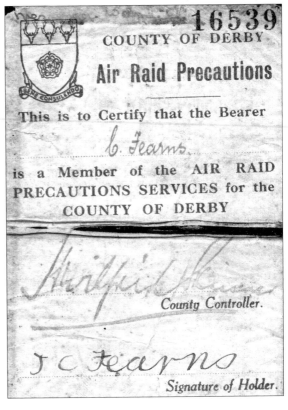

16539

COUNTY OF DERBY

Air Raid Precautions

This is to Certify that the Bearer

b. Fearns

is a Member of the AIR RAID PRECAUTIONS SERVICES for the COUNTY OF DERBY

County Controller.

J C Fearns

Signature of Holder.

moon is when you can read a newspaper by the light of the moon. It was on such a night that the big air-raid occurred. North Staffordshire and Derbyshire were covered with two or three inches of snow, so from the air it would probably look like a town, with the trees looking black, with no snow on them, enough for the enemy pathfinders to drop flares followed by hundreds of incendiary bombs to get fires going as markers for the heavy bombers following. But all the fire bombs did was to burn the church at Earl Sterndale out. Credit must be given to the local people for as soon as the incendiary bombs had stopped falling, they got shovels and spades to cover the bombs with snow and soil.

Ten minutes after the first wave had gone, the heavy bombers came, expecting to find their target ablaze. But all there was to greet them was a church on fire, which they might have thought was a decoy. As far as we know the only other building to be hit was the Bagshawe Arms. One of the small aluminium bombs hit the thick stone slates right above the oak beam; the slate held and the bomb bounced off, landing in the manure heap and burning itself out.

There were a lot of rumours going around as to what they were after. Some said the big dump at what we used to call McAlpines, up at Harpur Hill: others the viaducts at Millers Dale, while the old soldiers from the 1914-18 war claimed it would be the hundreds of tons of ammunition stockpiled along the sides of the byroads and lanes of the High Peak District.

We had now got twenty acres under plough and Uncle George managed to get a reaper and binder, an Albion no. 5. The man he bought it from unloaded it straight into the cornfield on Wormhill Moor. We had just finished opening it out, when the wagon arrived with the machine on, so they unloaded it with the tractor and started cutting right away. He showed Dad how to use it for half an hour, then said he would have to go, but wanted paying in cash before he went.

My Dad said he could have the £240 in sixpenny pieces if he wanted. He said it did not matter what it was so long as it was cash. At this point Uncle George took me home in his car to get the money ready.

The little man, who wore a bowler hat, stood talking to Dad for a while and then followed in his wagon to the Bagshawe Arms. By the time he arrived, Ma and I had got the money together and set out on the table all in six-penny pieces. Nine thousand and six hundred of them. 9,600 tanners!.

When Ma took the monthly takings into the bank, she always left the

Uncle Jim.

Cheedale.

tanners behind. When the little man came in, Ma gave him a drink and something to eat after which he approached the table and started counting his money. He had only got to about five pounds, when he suddenly said, *"Blow this"* and took off his bowler and swept all the coins into it, bid us good day and off he went to his wagon with me after him.

As he opened the cab door, I asked him for some luck money back. *"What do you mean?"* he said. *"Well, round here if we buy anything we always get some luck back to go with anything that we buy"*. With that he growled, reached a handful of tanners out of his hat and gave them to me, wishing us luck with the binder he had sold us. I thanked him and bid him good-bye and he was gone in a cloud of dust.

Harvesting at Wormhill.

Hard won milk

Some years later I was on a military exercise in the mid Wales Mountains, this being part of a REME workshop. We were on location as a forward recovery and repair team, consisting of 12 REME and 2 cooks. (The latter also doubled as labourers or anything else that was needed.) We had a good team.

We were miles from anywhere, but that did not matter as we had plenty of rations -what the army called ten-man packs of compo. These were very useful and contained most of the things you were likely to need. Indeed they were the envy of other armies, especially the USA, and that's saying something.

The only thing we were short of was fresh milk. Although there was plenty of dried milk, it made a lousy brew.

From time to time a Land Rover would need road testing after a repair. I would organise the craftsman who had carried out the repairs to take me out on a 'recce' around the local areas, where we tried to find a dairy farm of sorts, although it was not a dairy farming area.

This time we made our way five or six miles down the valley, where we came to a small farm with milk cows in the field. We entered the farmyard and I got out of the Land Rover to find a rough-looking lady. By saying 'rough', I mean that she had obviously worked hard manually all of her life. She looked at me surprised. I greeted her and informed her of our no-milk situation.

"Well," she replied, *"We can't sell you any, because we don't have a licence to sell milk."* I agreed with her, but then suggested that she could supply us with milk for a calf which we may have back at the camp. She informed us that she could sell us milk for a calf (although there was no doubt that she knew we had no calf) - this did make the sale legal.

"You'll have to wait until my husband comes off the top land. He won't be long," she said. She disappeared into the house, soon to reappear with two mugs of tea for us.

When the sound of a tractor could be heard approaching off the top land, two of the children went to fetch the cows in for milking. After a minute or two, a grey Ferguson tractor appeared, through the bed of the brook, the only way up and down this top ground.

When he reached the yard, he got off the "Fergy" and greeted us. His wife

Wormhill Hall.

Ancient field patterns at Blackwell, taken from Knotlow.

brought him out a mug of tea and explained to him what we wanted - and about the "calf". He smiled - he would be happy to fix us up once he had milked a couple of cows.

By now, the eight or so cows were going into the shippon (cow shed) to be fastened up and milked. A swarm of flies that had followed them down from the field was now buzzing around in a cloud outside the shippon door.

The farmer finished his brew; the children had collected him a clean milk bucket; all was set. He suddenly turned to me and announced, *"A strong young man like you should be able to milk your own."* *"Well, I can try,"* I replied, edging away. *"O.K., then; very good,"* he said, *"I'll get you a bucket and stool."*

Now me being a mere soldier and probably from a town, I thought he would give me an old quiet cow to learn on. Did he, heck! He handed me an old suckling bucket which had obviously been used for feeding calves for many years. He then gave me an old stool and led me to an evil-looking Welsh black. Although she was a heifer, she would have looked more at home in a Spanish bullring.

I weighed the situation up. Changing the old stool for a better one, I approached the heifer and dug my head into her side. This would put her off-balance should she decide to kick. I slapped the stool down, sitting on it in a manner which suggested I meant business. She tried to kick, but I managed to hold her with my left arm, drawing the milk out of her with my right. By the time I had finished milking her, she had relaxed and was quiet.

From the moment he gave me that old bucket, I knew that it was the farmer's intention to have a good laugh at me being unceremoniously kicked out. It turned out that the only way the farmer had managed to milk the heifer before was with the use of "barnacles", something which we never had used, as there would usually be two of us, if a cow was a known kicker.

"You've milked Welsh blacks before?" the farmer suggested. He had now milked another cow. He gave his wife the bucket of milk. She took the bucket and poured it through the cooler and gave us two gallons or so to take with us.

I enquired how much I owed the farmer for the milk. *"Nothing. Not after teaching me a lesson that I shouldn't take strangers for mugs. I won't take nothing for the milk."* He smiled.

"Come on," I told him, *"There's no taste in nowt and the bit of exercise did me good. You have to keep your hand in, don't you?"* Whereupon he gave

me a dry look. As we left I gave the kids a big tin containing 20 or 30 smaller tins of sweets and chocolates, about fourteen pound in weight. This pleased them no end as there was no money for such luxuries on those hill farms at that time.

Now realising what their windfall was, the older boy dashed towards the house to fetch a tin opener. I understood where he was going and called him back. *"Hey, why are you going for a tin opener? A big, strong lad like you doesn't need a tin opener. Give me that tin. I'll open it."*

Unknown to the children, I had a small military issue tin opener in my hand (another useful content of those ten-man packs of compo). I took the tin and opened it with the concealed tin opener. It looked as though I had opened it with my thumbnail - the children were so intent on the contents of the tin they were easily fooled. They were very impressed. To my surprise, instead of attacking the contents, the boy dashed off to his dad. *"Da! Da!"* shouted the excited Welsh voice, *"he's opened this tin with his thumbnail."* He showed his dad the tin and his dad smiled, puzzled. *"He did, Da. We saw him."*

I looked at my young colleague alongside me and, as we left, I said to him, *"At least we've left them with something to think about."*

"Me as well," he smiled.

Some of my Army memories.

Postscript

I am transported back in time to 1944. I am standing on a footbridge over the River Wye in Cheedale, watching men and boys working sheep into a fold by the old sheep wash. Two men are in the water up to their waists, each holding a sheep and washing their wool in the river, while two others are catching sheep in the fold, ready to pass to the washers. The water is cold so no time must be lost.

All was so peaceful down in that valley you would not think there was a war on. Above the noise of sheep washing, I thought I heard a faint rumbling. Yes! I heard it again, a little louder, coming from the North. Listening, I realised it was a train, changing from loud to soft as it plunged in and out of tunnels. It sounded very big and very fast. Suddenly, it burst out of the last tunnel before Miller's Dale, spitting sparks, fire and steam. The very valley was shaken by this monster train.

It was drawn by two of the largest steam locomotives, pulling wagons loaded with tanks, guns and all manner of weapons, and rail cars full of troops. Two more locomotives pushed it from behind. Reaching Miller's Dale the back locomotive slowed down and was shunted onto the North bound line to go back towards Stockport to help get another heavily laden troop train up over the High Peak Levels. But the troop train roared South, ever South, powered by those three locos, one green, one red and one blue. As they dispersed down the valley, I said to myself, *"They are coming, Mr. Hitler, and they are coming after YOU."*

D-day was upon us at last. We were all filled with adrenalin, from the land workers, who fed and clothed the nation, to the fighting forces at the sharp end who were putting their very lives on the line.